When God Writes Your Love Story

The ultimate approach to guy/girl relationships

Eric & Leslie Ludy

Multnomah®Publishers *Sisters, Oregon*

When God Writes Your Love Story
published by Multnomah Publishers, Inc.

Printed in the United States of America.

For information:
MULTNOMAH PUBLISHERS, INC.
POST OFFICE BOX 1720
SISTERS, OREGON 97759

03 04 05 06 07 - 13 12 11 10 9

Dedication

*For anyone who has
longed to sing the sweeter song*

Contents

5

Section Three
WAITING FOR A LOVE STORY

Section Four
SWEETENING A LOVE STORY

Section Five
DISCOVERING A GOD-WRITTEN LOVE STORY

Acknowledgments

The past four years have held challenges like we've never known before. Time and time again, you have provided a comforting refuge of encouragement, support, prayer, and most of all, unconditional love. The strength to share this message has come largely from all of you, our faithful family and friends who have upheld our arms throughout the battle...

Thank you:

Richard Runkles—for being like a sturdy anchor during the storms of life. For believing in us.

Janet Runkles—for your timely, motherly wisdom, for faithful prayers that God surely hears, and for riding the ups and downs right along with us. For being available to help us in any way we needed. For getting us organized!

David Runkles—for being an encouragement extraordinaire, for being an unchanging example of true integrity, and for being a wonderful friend and brother always.

John Runkles—for your "John" humor that always brings a smile, for your constant cheerfulness that rubs off on us, and being a wonderful friend and brother always.

Win Ludy—for sacrificing of yourself to give to us. For your uplifting attitude. For always being there. For keeping us entertained with "C.O.L's!" Hope you never change!

Barb Ludy—for your tireless, unhurried, listening ear. For your "Barb" hugs and your incredible example of joy in each day.

Mark Ludy—for just being "Marky" and adding sunshine and hilarity to our world! We love you and appreciate you so much! Thanks for sharing your enthusiasm for life with us.

Kristina Ludy—for living out the words of St. Francis of Assisi: *Preach Christ at all times, and if necessary use words*. We are amazed and inspired by your simple yet profound faith! We dearly love you!

Dave Wolf—a true and faithful friend, willing to stand beside through not only the joy, but especially the pain…an amazing example of selfless giving. For *your* C.O.L's! (You're on your way to the pros!)

Ann Freeman—for always providing a heavenly perspective and for somehow always knowing when we needed prayer.

Ryan and Molly Gold—for the laughter and late night chats! Thanks for refreshing us with His love.

Dawn Hawley—you had a vision for this message from the very beginning and your prayer has carried us so many times. God has used you mightily in our lives. Thank you.

Mary Jo Gentert—it's too bad we can't clone you and give you as a gift to everyone we know! You bring a bright light of sunshine to an office that can too often become routine.

Tom Hovostol—our wonderful pastor and friend, for taking time from your busy schedule and giving counsel and encouragement…for showing such genuine interest in our lives…you have been more of a blessing that you can know.

Leslie:
Searching for True Love

think we should break up," he softly said. Those were the words I'd been dreading for months. "I'm ready to start seeing other people."

My trembling fingers tightened around the phone cord, and I choked back the sob that threatened to explode from my tightening lungs. There was a long, awkward pause as he waited for me to speak. My only consolation was that he could not see my pale face. I would never have been able to hide my devastated expression had he been in the room at that heart-wrenching moment.

The nightmare had come true...again. What had started out as a harmless, fun, innocent relationship had slowly become a complicated entanglement of emotion and passion, only to end abruptly now that the fire had faded. The cutting pain that ruthlessly squeezed my heart was so intense I could scarcely breathe. Somehow, I managed to end the phone call with at least a small amount of dignity. As I placed the receiver into its cradle, a dark cloud of despair overcame me, mercilessly pouring a violent torrent of rejection and hopelessness into my reeling mind.

It was over. Once again, I was in for a sleepless night of agony, hours of weeping until no more tears would come. Once again, I would have to face the aching, desperate loneliness of walking into a crowded room full of strangers—with no hand to hold, no strong arm to gently rest on my back and give me security. Once again, I was alone.

How many years had I longed and urgently searched for true love? How many nights had I laid awake, dreaming of a beautiful romance—a lasting relationship that *wouldn't* end in heartache?

I had made incredible sacrifices in an attempt to somehow cling to every short-lived dating relationship that came my way. I had given pieces of myself away to each man that came into my life—pieces of my heart, my emotions, and even my body. Yet, once he had tired of me, my fragile heart would be played with and then carelessly tossed aside. Even if I was the one who ended a relationship, the heartbreaking pain was inevitable. Every time it felt like something precious was being violently ripped from inside of me.

I yearned to be loved and cherished. I had dreamed of a perfect love story for my entire life. But somewhere in the midst of the endless cycle of one temporary romance after the next, my dreams had shattered right along with the broken and fragmented pieces of heart.

I had asked others for advice. Those from the older generation had simply given guidelines to follow, which were so completely out of touch with the reality of my world that they were worthless to me. As a Christian, I had listened carefully to the instructions given by the church leaders, and tried to follow the Christian rules of dating to the letter. But their rules never protected me from a broken heart and shattered life.

When I turned to those in the younger generation, I found they were all in the same boat I was in—an endless cycle of shallow and cheap romances that never lasted and left us emotionally bleeding and insecure. In fact, the pain *I* experienced was small compared to what many of my friends had gone through.

As I lay on my bed pondering these thoughts, I found myself inwardly forming a desperate prayer.

"God, where are You in this?" my heart cried silently. "I am Your child. All my life, You know I have longed for something beautiful. I have searched for true love. Does a pure and perfect romance even exist in this dark world of lust and perversion and sin? Should I even dare to dream of something beyond the shallow, meaningless, cheap version of love I've known so far?"

Then came a soft, gentle tugging upon my heart. Suddenly I somehow knew that my life did not need to be this way and that God had something better for me. It was almost as if God himself was reminding me...*I Am the Author of True Love; I Am the Creator of Romance.*

A quiet challenge deeply touched my spirit in that moment, as if God were tenderly standing before me, with tears of boundless love in His eyes, whispering to my heart...*You have searched for true love in your own way. But My ways are not your ways. I want to script a beautiful tale just for you, but first you must trust Me with the pen of this precious area of your life. Will you let Me write your love story?*

It wasn't too long after that tear-filled, hopeless night that my unforgettable journey began. It was a journey to discover something I never before knew existed—the matchless beauty of a God-written love story. More out of desperation than confidence, I invited the Creator of the Universe to be the center of my love life. Did He disappoint me? Quite the opposite. I was soon to discover that my most Faithful Friend in the entire world, who loved me more than I could comprehend, had a plan for my love life that would take my breath away with its beauty.

I don't know if I could ever fully convey the awesome wonder of what it was like to have a God-written love story. During my entire romance with Eric, I was so aware of the fact that it was *God* who was leading each step, guiding each conversation, painting each sunset, and standing over us with a smile. The cheap, imitation romance I'd known before simply could not be compared to this new kind of love I had discovered. I was daily amazed that I had come from a place of heartbreak, confusion, and compromise in relationships, to a dream come true. I had discovered a kind of divine love that can't even be found in the fairy-tales, simply by giving God the pen of my life's story and allowing Him to write each chapter. He was interested in this part of my life. He did have a plan! And He has one for you, too.

> *As for God, His way is perfect.*
> Psalm 18:30 NEW INTERNATIONAL VERSION

This book is guaranteed to change your life. Please join Eric and me as we share this unforgettable journey which God took us on to discover what a God-written love story is all about. We have attempted to share these excerpts from our lives as candidly as possible. And by the way, when it matters, some places and people's names have been changed and physical descriptions altered to protect certain individual privacy.

As you read this book, you may cry with us, laugh with us, laugh *at* us, even get mad at us along the way—but we hope you will hang in there till the final chapter and discover something beyond what you've ever dreamed of. Through the pages of this book, it is our hope and prayer that you will discover the secret to finding true love...a God-written love story.

This book is *not* about rules, relationship how-tos, or a comprehensive guide to experiencing the singles' scene.

Rather, this book is all about an invitation to *you*. The One who knows you better than you know yourself, and who loves you more than you can comprehend, wants to take *you* on a journey.

This journey is for anyone who is searching for the beauty of true and lasting love, for romance in its purest form, and is willing to do whatever it takes in order to find it. This journey is for anyone who has made mistakes, whether small or big, and said, "It's too late for me," to discover *that* kind of love. It's a journey for anyone who is tired of the same old scene of physically intense relationships, devoid of meaning and purpose.

This journey is for anyone who will dare to dream beyond the cheap and diluted romance our culture offers and hold out for an infinitely better way. This journey is even for the skeptic, who doubts that such a way exists.

No matter where you are or where you have been...*this invitation is for you.* The very One who is the Author of all true love and romance is standing before you, asking you gently,

Will you let Me write your love story?

If you will trust Him enough to give Him the pen of your life, you are in for a journey that will forever spoil you for the ordinary. It's a journey on which you will discover perfect love and pure romance as it was *truly* intended to be.

Section One
Desiring a Love Story

Chapter One

Eric:

The Babes and the Big Egos

All the Kens and Barbies sat around the table. Amid glistening smiles, moussed hairdos, and Coppertone tans, the fragrance of Polo, with a hint of Skin-So-Soft wafted through the café booth. I nibbled at my burrito as the conversation around me finally arrived at its ultimate destination.

"So, Kevin?" Barbie #1 flirted across the table, "Tell us who you're seeing now."

Kevin was used to having eyes upon him. Being a Tom Cruise look-a-like in the early nineties has a way of boosting the ol' ego. Having a senator for a dad didn't hurt either. While crunching a chip between perfect teeth, an "I thought you'd never ask" smirk found its way across his face.

As all of us camp counselors leaned in, eyes bulging with expectancy, Kevin finally revealed the secret in a low monotone, "Her name is…Sandra!"

This only added to the excitement and wonder, because no one had any idea who Sandra was.

"Is she a babe?" begged the resident Brad Pitt, alias Mike from Wyoming.

Say no more! Swift as the bionic man, Kevin whipped out his wallet. Moments later we all observed a photograph of the "Babe of the Century," as Tom Cruise wanna-be so proudly referred to her.

"Ooooh!" was heard from the corner of the table where Brad Pitt and Leo DiCaprio, (Wayne from Denver), were discussing the finer points of her femininity.

"*I* think she has a huge nose!" grumbled two of the super models under their breath.

I continued to pick at my burrito.

Barbie # 2, sitting beside Top Gun, was next in the heartthrob inquisition. The photo was removed to shouts of, "You go girl!" from the Barbies, and low disapproving rumbles about his skinny neck from the Kens, Brads, Leos, and Toms.

After a week of having to exhibit saint-like behavior to all the little campers, and being super-spiritual while around the camp leaders, it was time to let our hair down— time to let the real passions of life come out. I mean, in your late teens and early twenties, you can sing only so many spiritual camp songs before you need an infusion of good old-fashioned romance!

One year prior, it was talks like this that really lit my fire. I use to love to brag about my love life at camp and exaggerate about *my* "Babe of the Century" in a way that would make all the guys jealous and all the girls insecure. You could say just about anything and get away with it; no one was going home with you to check out your story.

I used to crave these love chats, but something about Eric Ludy (alias Pee-Wee Herman in *this* group) had changed—something big—something that made me want to slide under the table when all those inquisitive eyes turned my way.

I'll never forget that moment! There I was, my fork picking at the jalapeno stranded on the corner of my plate and my mind screaming over and over in my head, *"Please don't ask me…please don't ask me."* Well…they asked.

"So Eric? Tell us about your exciting love life!"

All the periwinkle, emerald, and dark brown eyeballs were twinkling at me with expectation. I gulped.

"Uhhhh," I mumbled. My palms were sweaty. My tongue was dry and thick, like I had a felt eraser in my mouth. Finally, Pee-Wee Herman spoke up. "Uhh, I uhh, actually, uh, I am waiting on God."

But, to be honest, it didn't really come out as clearly as I just wrote it. The last part of my sentence was mumbled under my breath sounding something like, "Ima waying on Gaw."

I hoped I could answer quickly and have them move on to Elle McPherson, seated next to me, poised and ready with a photo of her hunk. *The plan backfired!* They became even *more* interested!

"Uh, I *think* we missed that, Ludy!" Tom Cruise sarcastically challenged, "Was that a girl's name or your favorite Chinese food?"

After the laughs subsided, I began again, this time a little more clearly.

"I know this may sound strange, you guys, but I've decided that I won't give my heart to another girl until God shows me it's my wife!"

I have often wished I could have been more eloquent, that I could have made my resolve sound a little more appealing to my audience, now staring with mouths ajar. But I guess God wanted me to know that I was following a different path, *not* for the approval of the Kens and the Barbies of this world, but simply to honor and love Him.

It was a lonely moment. Silence filled our corner of the restaurant, and all eyes focused on the jalapeno I was ruthlessly stabbing to death.

"That's...*interesting*!" Super-model, Kayla, awkwardly noted as her eyes grew large with disbelief.

"Oh, give me a *break!* How in the world do you expect to find someone, Ludy, if you're not out there looking?" Leonardo chimed in, accompanied by "yeahs" and "exactlys" from around the café booth.

After a moment of reflective silence, I took a deep breath and stated, "I believe that if God wants me to be married" (another deep breath), "He will pick her out for me."

A dark cloud settled over the entire group and rained down bewilderment and shock in the form of ghostlike faces and rolled eyes. I glanced up from my tortured jalapeno to discover a long bony index finger pointing at me, about twelve inches from my nose. Kevin used that finger like Clint Eastwood used a gun. He didn't shoot to maim—he shot to *kill!* Kevin's bronzed features had taken on a deep shade of red and his lips were bubbling like a lava pool ready to explode. After three long seconds, he finally erupted.

"I totally disagree with you!" He fumed with his index finger still targeting my right nostril. "God doesn't want us hanging around nagging Him about something like *that!*"

A few "amens" from the crowd textured his passionate sermon. He continued...

"I believe God wants *us* to pick," he preached, "and then He blesses *our* choice!" He paused and then came to a climactic finish, "It's sappy Christianity like yours that gives us Christians the image of helpless orphans! It is absolutely *ridiculous* to think that God would care that much about *your* love life!"

The finger held fast for another few long seconds, then slowly dropped as if to say, *"You show any sign of life, and I'll shoot again!"*

I was the ultimate bummer to their titillating conversation. If ever you want to drain the juice right out of romance, just bring *God* into the picture. I had committed the unpardonable camp counselor sin, and all the eyes around the table were letting me know it.

While growing up I got along with everybody. I knew how to hang with the crowd and not offend anyone. I was careful to say the right thing in order to avoid disagreements. Eric Ludy had never been known for his backbone, well, except maybe when it came to the Denver Broncos. But when it came to things that *really* mattered, I was a serious wimp! This was one of the first times in my life I can remember actually standing up for something I believed in (that wasn't orange and blue).

Ironically, I didn't even know exactly what I was talking about. Just twelve months before, I, too, would have "totally disagreed" with what I had just said. But over the past year, God was challenging me to apply my Christianity to *every* area of my life. Was it ridiculous to think God would be interested in my love life enough to lead me and provide a wife for me?

I shifted in my seat, stabbed my jalapeno one last time and spoke. "All I know," I said, "is that every time *I* have tried to pick a girl out for my life, I realize in the long run that I have *horrible* taste."

Everyone wanted to chuckle, but everything was still a little too serious for that.

All eyes were wide and all ears were open in wonder and bewilderment as I concluded. "Kevin, if God had ten women line up in front of me and said, 'Eric you pick!' I would fall flat on my face before Him and say, 'God you know me better than I know myself...*You pick!*'"

I bet no one present other than myself remembers that moment. To them it was probably just the ramblings of a lunatic named Ludy. But for me it was a defining moment. It was almost as if God was saying, "How seriously are you going to trust Me, son?"

So there it was, in front of the babes and the big egos that God challenged me to officially trust Him with the "pen" of my life. I had held onto that pen for twenty years, and now over a chicken burrito and a mangled jalapeno, I handed it over to the great Author to allow Him to work His wonder.

Chapter Two

Eric:
In Search of
a Sweeter Song

*A generation's longing
for a better kind of love*

Homecoming 1988 was a disaster! It was my senior year in high school, and some whacko played upon my gullibility and convinced me that in October Jesus would return and the end of the world would come.

I hear you saying, "And you believed him?" Well, I'd like to blame it on the education system for not teaching me how to use my brain. But...yes! I believed him!

Due to the fact that the world was only weeks away from total devastation, I had to put my priorities right in my life. The homecoming dance was a month away and a good majority of the girls were still available.

"I'm not even going to be around for *that,"* I reasoned to myself as the weeks ticked away. The problem was, *not only* did the weeks pass by, but so did all the available dates from my school. That would not have posed a difficulty though, if *all* the available dates in October, *after Jesus was supposed to have come and gone*, hadn't passed by, *too!*

Well, life would just have to continue. The homecoming dance could go on without ol' dateless Eric...except for one small problem. My crazy classmates pulled a cruel stunt and put me on the Homecoming Court. I guess they felt a Pee-Wee Herman would be a nice finishing touch to an otherwise machismo lineup of studly football player nominees. Now I *had* to go! And I had to have a *date!*

I found a girl in a nearby town that was a friend of a friend. She agreed, rather reluctantly, to be my date for the evening. But she made sure that I knew, "The fact that I'm going with you to this dance doesn't mean anything beyond going to this dance, I hope you know!"

She was a curly-headed brunette, heavy on perfume and light on the charm. My first mistake was forgetting her at the dance and losing her for about an hour. The second mistake I made sort of sealed my fate for the evening. It was all very innocent. There I was, fumbling around trying to somehow apologize for my terrible absence of sensitivity. I mean, I hadn't just forgotten that she was with me that night, I had totally forgotten that she *existed*. A girl actually came up to me and informed me,

"LouAnn is furious with you!"

I innocently replied, "Who's LouAnn?"

So there I was, brainless as a paperweight and red as a beet, trying to convince her that she was important to me.

"LouAnn!" I floundered, "You are great! You are special!"

A snort of disgust blew from her nostrils. Then came my demise. Over the next few minutes, my buddies began to crowd around and the nature of the conversation began to brighten. A few jokes were made and all of us were laughing, well, all except LouAnn. My buddy Darren brought up the subject of names, and we were chuckling about how all of us sort of take on an appearance that fits our names. That was my cue. The brilliant Don Juan that I am, I turned my gaze toward my beautiful brunette and spoke.

"It's kinda hilarious, but did I tell you...I've got a cat named LouAnn?!"

Her response was anything but froth with frolicking romance. Her eyes turned a shade of neon green that I have never again witnessed. It was before she officially kissed me goodnight with a right hook (or did I just imagine that part?) that she said something like,

"Yeah? Well, I have a pug-nosed dog named Eric!"

The Beautiful Side of Love

Most of us have fallen flat on our faces when it comes to romance. Nearly all of us are familiar with the awful fragrance that accompanies a decomposing relationship.

As Joel, a college friend, said after he had crashed and burned once again on a Saturday night,

"Man! I know how to start the relationships; I just don't know how to keep 'em."

That, unfortunately, is not an isolated problem to Joel from third floor Baker Hall (who, by the way, is still single as of the last romance update). In our generation it is a problem of epidemic proportions.

Then there is Margo from Minnesota. Margo doesn't feel much sympathy for Joel. As she would say, "I wish I even had the *opportunity* to mess up a relationship with a guy!"

Whether you identify with Joel or with Margo or neither, I guarantee you will identify with the sentiments of Katie, a senior in college who has done a lot of thinking on the subject.

"Eric, you need to understand," Katie exclaims with a cute little voice, "I want my love life to be *beautiful!*"

Katie represents the sentiments of her entire love-hungry generation weaned on condoms and AIDS education. We *know* the biology, but we do *not* know "the beautiful side of love."

If we were to be honest, most of us concluded by the age of sixteen that the "beautiful side of love" is something only discovered on a Hollywood movie set by folks like Tom Hanks and Meg Ryan. The "happily ever after" stuff is for idealists and dreamers, not realists and critical thinkers.

Now I want you to know up front that I am *not* passing myself off as the Romance Doctor. I can hear Leslie now,

"He's right about that!" (But, I do have my moments!)

I climbed out of the same culture you did. I grew up on *Dukes of Hazard* and played with a Slinky. I wore Levi's Shrink-to-Fits and Nike sportswear. I was in elementary school when we ran out of gas in the world, in junior high when we discovered more, and had just left high school when we bombed Iraq so we wouldn't run out again.

I know the world you live in, because I live in it too. And though I didn't get a doctoral degree in romance, I believe I have a message that can turn your concept of a love life upside down. If you are anything like the rest of our love-hungry generation, you are going to discover a little taste of heaven on earth when you read about the "beautiful side of love" that *really does* exist.

If you knew my love life history, it might cause you to wonder what qualifies me to share this beautiful side of love with you. I often wonder the very same thing. From the beginning, I was quite inept at this relationship thing. Back in the good ol' days when I was a pimply-faced and pubertized thirteen-year-old, I wondered why a girl would ever even want me. Maybe some of you never went through the "Oh, God, have mercy and save the world from my face!" stage of development, but for those of you who did...I can identify.

I had my gangly four-eyed and brace-faced season of struggle, when I was termed by all the well-meaning women in my life as "skinny" and in desperate need of one of their meals. I remember trying Selsen Blue (super-medicated formula) for the nerdy white flakes speckled throughout my hairdo. Of course, when my younger brother, Marky, found the blue bottle hidden under my bed, he transformed into Frank Sinatra and serenaded me with a nauseating rendition of *White Christmas*...in October.

No one can accuse me of not knowing what it feels like to be ugly! I remember getting a free photo shoot from Olan Mills when I was in the height of puberty. *They* paid *me* to take the one free photo just so it would not end up in their example album by mistake.

Yes, I also know what it is like to be lonely. Really lonely! In fact, I understand the toxic mix of loneliness and sexual longing that creates the sensation of your heart being toasted like a s'more-destined marshmallow over a roaring campfire.

I know what it is like to want someone to hold, someone to gently lean upon me, someone to care about my needs in, you know, a romantic sort of way! I know what it is like to desire someone with whom I could share my wild life, my passionate love, and my intimate embrace. I know what it is like to long for "the beautiful side of love."

Homecoming 1988 was a disaster. There was nothing "beautiful" about it! (I'm still a little insecure when people talk about pug-nosed dogs around me.) But wedding date 1994 was off the charts incredible! Somewhere between homecoming and honeymoon my entire understanding of love changed. And in the process, I discovered what is missing in our generation's concept of love and romance. I discovered "the beautiful side of love." And it was found in a very unexpected place!

The Passion and the Pew

Growing up in the church, I came to believe that everything I longed for was somehow bad for my proper spiritual development. "THOU SHALT NOT!" the pastor would boom from the pulpit as I sat in the rear-numbing pew daydreaming about sexy Suzie McFrougal from Hank's Burger Barn. For most of my life, I thought it was *God* who posed the greatest hurdle to experiencing all the thrills of love and romance. And I would have taken great offense to someone trying to convince me that God should have a greater role in my love story. All the stern "thou shalt nots" He had so thoughtfully bestowed on me were quite enough, thank you!

For many years of my life, I struggled to find the right words to capture my agonizing frustrations. I was a young man fighting a constant inward battle between needing to obey God's "thou shalt nots" and yet longing to fulfill my passionate, sensual desires.

It wasn't until I stumbled upon the following story from Greek legend that I found the perfect picture to describe my years of torment. If *you* have unsuccessfully tried to mix "the passion" with "the pew," there's a good chance that you will be able to relate to the hidden message in this Greek-tale-with-a-Ludy-twist.

The Sweet Song Beckons
(Based on Homer's *Odyssey*)

Captain Ulysses cut a powerful figure as he stood on the deck of his great ship. The afternoon sun shimmered off the water as the he strode about the ship with grace and dignity. Ulysses' every move was carefully observed by the helmsman who labored long and hard for nothing more than the approving eye of his noble captain.

"Steady as she goes!" Ulysses boomed, his voice filling the salty air.

"Yes, sir!" was the helmsman ready reply.

After giving the command, the captain turned his iron gaze to starboard side where land was just now coming into view. Neither the screeching gulls overhead, nor the rhythmic splash of water against the ship's side diverted Ulysses attention from what lay just ahead. The smell of adventure was in the air; everything was just as Ulysses liked it. Then, amidst his reverie came a voice arresting his attention.

"Captain!"

The noble leader quickly turned to find a worried seaman, eyes filled with trepidation and lips rattling with anxiety.

"Captain!" He again blared, his whole face ablaze with horror.

"Settle down!" Ulysses softly commanded, "Take a deep breath and tell me what's the matter!"

The entire crew within earshot had stopped and gathered round to hear the outcome of this all-important conversation.

"Uh...we...ah...!" he stuttered, "well...uh...you see, sir!"

Ulysses grabbed him by the collar, yanked him within inches of his furrowed brow and demanded, "Come on lad, if you value your life, speak!"

The drama built as the petrified first mate raised a quivering finger due north and stuttered, "The Sirens, sir!"

Ulysses' face drew tight and a woeful sigh was heard about the ship. The Siren mermaids were just ahead, ready to sing their irresistibly enchanting song and cause the bewitched sailors to steer their vessel onto the rocks. The song of the Sirens was so sweet, so alluring, no red-blooded man could resist it. Ulysses had to act quickly—*while wisdom still remained.*

"Those devilish mermaids won't get us!" he announced to his fearful crew. "That's right! That lovely, luscious, melodious music played by those beautiful mermaids won't have its way with us. No ship wreck for us today, lads!"

But even as Ulysses pondered the intoxicating music, he felt his wisdom slipping. He was gripped by a magnetic urge to hear just a short strain of the legendary song of the mermaids.

"Maybe we could try and miss the rocks? NO!" He chided himself, "NO! It does this to all captains who pass by. They all *think* they can resist, but then lose their senses and follow the sweet music to their deaths upon the jagged rocks, while the mermaids scoff from above. NO!"

Ulysses ran to the bow of the ship, turned and bellowed for all the crewmen to hear.

"We are mere men, unable to resist the promise of sweet love in the mermaid's song. The Sirens have baited every ship before us with their songs, and every time the ships have crashed against the rocks upon which the Sirens sit. But not this time, my friends. *We* will not fall to their temptation; indeed, we will not even allow ourselves to be tempted!"

"I want every sailor to take some of this bee's wax and put it in your ears so you can hear nothing. And tie *me* to the mast!"

His crew looked at each other in bewilderment.

"You heard me!" He shouted again, "Tie me to the mast! And tie me tight and fast!"

The sun angrily beat down as the disciplined crew rushed about the ship responding to Ulysses' orders. And none too soon had they crammed the wax into their ears and finished tying their Captain to the mast, but the beautiful and intoxicating love song of the Siren mermaids began to softly fill the air. The Sirens' song, in all its passion and wonder, greeted the ship across the water as a warm fire greets cold hands on a winter's day.

The crew was oblivious—all except Ulysses who, while tied to the mast, had no wax to stop the music. Ulysses' blood ran hot with passion. "Untie me!" he screamed in anguish, "Please untie me! I command you to untie me…please, I beg you."

But the crewmen could not hear and had been commanded not to read his lips. The song grew louder and lovelier, and Ulysses groaned with sheer physical desire. He then began to scream like a madman for someone to heed his orders and turn the ship towards the source of that sweet, lustful music. Ulysses threatened the plank, Cyclops feedings, and various other forms of torture as the ship passed the Sirens' rocky coastline, and then finally beyond the reach of their song.

An exhausted Ulysses, his face a deep scarlet from the struggle, finally was untied and fell limp upon the ship's deck.

"Why?" he moaned with his remaining strength, "Why does it seem that the things I desire most in this life lead to my destruction? Why must I be restrained from something so beautiful? The mast is my savior this day from my headlong craving for that sweet but deadly song of the Siren mermaids!"[1]

Rope Burned?

I feel Ulysses' pain! I grew up being taught how to "tie myself to the mast" while listening to the song of temptation at full volume. I heard all the fire and brimstone sermons on "the rocks of death!" I had all the manuals on enduring rope burn, and I even had one called "How to Chart Your Course So You Never Hear or See a Mermaid."

I also lost my senses a few times during my horribly extended pubertized years. I was sort of a Houdini, with the way I could slip out of the rope and escape from that mast without any of the National Guard finding out. Not only was I a magician when it came to discovering loopholes in the ropes, but I was a lot like a two-year-old driving a semi when it came to steering my ship away from the rocks. I became a seasoned professional at the fine art of incurring serious boat damage.

Like most guys, I grew up in the boy's locker room. The singular topic of conversation that cluttered the airwaves made it a *very* educational place. I learned far more about my sexuality in two minutes standing next to Donny Lucero's locker, than I did in *two hours* of scientific lecturing from my dad the night he took me for a drive in our banana-yellow VW bus and gave me…"The Talk."

I had a raging desire within me to have a female companion, someone I could love and be loved by, some one I could be intimate with. The difference between Donny Lucero's advice and the advice I received from my church on the subject was shocking. Ten bucks says you could guess whose advice I preferred.

I wanted to experience *all* that Donny described. I wanted to understand it, and *not* just in theory! The problem was, when I came into church and sat down in my pew, I always heard the same thing...THOU SHALT NOT! And "thou shalt nots" only go so far on a hormone-infested young man who's looking for loopholes in the rope so he can accidentally-on-purpose steer his love boat as close to the rocks as he can possibly get.

If you are anything like me, by the age of twenty you are sinking on the high seas, and you have more water *in* your boat then there is outside your boat. Maybe you are so debilitated with frustration, so sore with rope burn, and so sick and tired of listening to the exploits of *your own* personal Donny Lucero, that the next person who offers you a "thou shalt not," *thou shalt pop* them one right in the old smackeroo!

We all agree that this rope burn stuff really stinks, but is there any other way to keep us from crashing against the rocks? Thankfully, the story does *not* end here. Greek legend also tells us that another ship passed that way. And the captain of that ship responded to the Sirens very differently than Ulysses.

The Sweeter Song

Not far behind the ship of Ulysses, came another great ship. These sailors also realized the dangers of the Sirens and the rocks upon which they sat.

"Captain Orpheus," the first mate enthusiastically declared, "the sweet song of the Sirens lies just ahead!"

With that announcement, the crew cheered and the great Orpheus smiled. All around the ship, crewmen's voices rang with excitement. The part of the voyage that they longed for was soon at hand. In fact, there were some on the ship who had come along *just* to hear the music.

With a knowing smile, the dauntless Captain received a beautifully adorned case from his cabin boy. The acclaimed Orpheus carefully removed the priceless instrument as the crewmen stood nearby with bated breath. Then, with princely grace, he lifted the instrument above his head with a gesture of victory, while the crew around him whistled with enthusiasm.

"Play it, Captain!" cheered the helmsman.

"Come on, great Captain Orpheus, play it!" whooped the enthusiastic first mate.

All eyes were transfixed upon their hero. Captain Orpheus took his stance and began to masterfully play the most perfect music men's ears had ever heard. Each crewman became lost in the reverie of the song.

All too soon the Siren coastline was out of sight and the Master musician concluded the song that he himself had composed. Not a single man aboard ship was tempted by the Sirens' melody. In fact, no one even noticed it. Though the mermaid's music was alluring and sweet, the superb Orpheus played for his crew...*a sweeter song.*[2]

A Different Tune

For those of us who have spent years tied to the mast and for those of us who couldn't bear the allurement and crashed against the rocks, it's time to set sail to a different tune.

In our love-hungry generation we struggle to believe that the "beautiful side of love" really exists. But the truth is, Hollywood *can't even touch* the version of love that is alive and real and in the heart and mind of God. It is the "sweeter song." And when you hear this "sweeter song" you, too, will realize that it is ten thousand times more magnificent than your most grandiose imagination.

God created us with a desire for companionship. He designed us to *intensely* long for intimacy—spiritual, emotional, and yes, *even* physical. He did not make us this way and provide us with these longings as a form of cruel torture, but as the most perfect gift He could possibly give us. Just as a lover desires to show his adoration to his bride by tenderly presenting her with a delicate and fragrant rose, so has our Great Lover gifted us with this delicate and wondrous capacity to give and receive love and passion. And once we awaken to this truth, then we will also discover that, as the Inventor of romance, He also wants to teach us how to discover it in all its fullness.

So for all of you in this generation who dream of something eternally sweet and are tired of rope burn, God is eagerly waiting for you to jump aboard His ship so that He can play the "sweeter song" just for you.

A Step Further

Hunker down in a big overstuffed chair by a crackling fire and pull out your trusty Bible. Open it up to the book called The Song of Songs. If you read this book with the intention of discovering more about the nature of your God in heaven, then you will undoubtedly be caught up in the realization that He is the ultimate romantic.

Chapter Three

Eric:

Who's Captain of Your Love Boat?

*Laying the foundation
for a God-written love story*

Pouring Concrete

If you were building a house and you had brains, you would *not* want to build it on a mound of sand. Every wise and sensible builder would first dig a hole and pour some concrete. Jesus even makes this clear in Matthew chapter 7 when He talks about the "wise" and the "foolish" builders. Because, if a house is going to endure the storms of life, whether they be spiritual or tropical, it must have a foundation. Well, the same is true with a love life!

Let me take you on a little adventure into the land of concrete! It's not terribly romantic (the color gray never is) but it *is* terribly important. As you begin to read these next few pages, you may even begin to think, "What in the world does this have to do with my love life?"

Well, just hold on to your little hat and you'll discover that it has *everything* to do with your love life. In fact, as we will explain later in this book, it *is* your love life! It's the foundation of all success in relationships. To be prepared to relate to a member of the opposite sex, you must first learn how to relate to the *Creator* of the opposite sex.

Allow these words to sink deeply into your heart and mind, because if you miss them, you will have missed the secret key to unlocking the "sweeter song." And the "beautiful side of love" that you are longing for, will forever remain but a fairy-tale—somewhere beyond reality and your grasp.

How a Sweeter Love Story Begins

A great story in Christian history is about the apostle Andrew, one of Jesus' twelve disciples. Andrew was brought in before the governor Egeas to be reproved for his constant preaching of the controversial message of Jesus. The governor threatened, "If you don't stop preaching this message of Jesus and this cross, I'm going to crucify you on one, too!"[1] I don't know about you, but it would be very tempting at such a point for me to blurt out, "No problem! You want me to shut up? Zip! My lips are closed! Now, why don't we just forget about this cross thingamajig!"

Andrew, though, was undaunted and simply replied, "Sir, I would not have preached about the glory of the cross of Jesus if I was also not willing to die upon it!"

Andrew was immediately taken out and crucified. He was ruthlessly tied to two beams of splintery wood and set upright to die a slow and painful death. He hung there, in what must have been excruciating pain, for three days, preaching the triumphant message of Jesus and *His* cross the whole while; until he was finally taken home to be with the One he loved more than his very life.

I don't know about you, but growing up I never saw anything like *that*! I mean, that type of love for Christ, that type of passion for following Him, that type of abandonment of life! I had been a Christian for nearly two decades and some serious doubt had begun to creep into my mind regarding the accuracy of some of these legendary stories of the faith.

"If following Christ is really like *that*, then how come I never see anyone live like that today?" my little pea-brain would wonder.

I used to just accept what I heard in Sunday school. After all, it was Mrs. Puddlemeister, the esteemed Sunday school teacher who said it. How could *she* be wrong? But something caused me to stop accepting. Maybe it was the fact that I was constantly told by my school teachers that God wasn't there. Maybe it had something to do with the flimsy moral backbones of many of the people in my life who referred to themselves as Christians. Or maybe it was simply that I came to the point in my life where I wanted to go beyond "accepting" and truly *know* for myself, experientially, what I believed in.

Whatever it was, it invited a little mouse of cynicism into my head. And this pesky little rodent scurried around and nibbled away at my innocence and child-like faith. Though my parents and Mrs. Puddlemeister had taught me well, I became a doubter that such extravagant love for Jesus could be real, a doubter that Jesus was really Someone who people would be willing to die for.

That little mouse of cynicism is very common in our generation. For the most part, it has nibbled away at the very concept of who God is and who He wants to be in our lives. What I realized is that God *is real* whether *I* believe He is or not. And the day I recognized that, my nettlesome little mouse was caught in an industrial-sized rat trap.

The Aged Romanian

My younger brother, Marky, had a video that he described as, "Eric, this is the most incredible thing you will *ever* see or hear!" If you knew my brother, you would know why, at first, I rolled my eyes. My brother, Marky, is known as the Great Overstater. And he didn't come by his name because of just a few over-magnifications of the truth. I mean when Marky overstresses a point, he *really* stretches it! This is the same guy that "died and is plucking a harp next to St. Peter," after he ate a gourmet mushroom. This is the same guy who said, "I have never been so emotionally moved in all my twenty-three years on this planet," after seeing the movie *Babe*.

The Great Overstater was now waving a cheap looking video in front of my face and assuring me that this would be the most incredible thing I would *ever* see or hear. Well, even though it's hard for me to admit that the Great Overstater could actually be right, when he pushed the play button what I witnessed was truly incredible!

Onto the fuzzy thirteen inch screen came a weary old man with a face full of wrinkles. I'll never forget hearing his elderly voice shake as he started off his short little talk. His body looked tired and decrepitly old, yet his eyes radiated a fire and gentleness I had never in my life seen.

Even though as an older brother I was supposed to act nonchalant about something my brother was excited about, I couldn't help but be drawn in. I waited upon every word this wrinkled man spoke as if he were giving me the secret code to unlocking the mysteries of the universe. And in a way...he was!

In all my growing up years of being a Christian, my eyes had never seen something so worthy of my respect, my ears had never heard anything so sweet and tender, and my heart had never burned so desperately to know Jesus better.

"My Sweet Jesus!" He uttered with his eyes turned heaven-ward.

I almost expected God to reach down and take him home right then. How could the Shepherd of souls resist intimately embracing such a lover? This old withered saint was like a child as he spoke to God. He was different than the preachers

I had heard from the pulpit and the dynamic speakers I had heard on the radio. His words penetrated my heart. He was strangely soft and if I could say, even beautiful. His very presence seemed to reach out to me as he spoke and offer me a great big hug.

I found my tough manly eyes filled with tears as he haltingly shared about his greatest Love. He said things I had heard before, but it was the sincerity, the gentleness with which he uttered them that touched my soul. He spoke of his life in Romania under Communist dictatorship, his absolute surrender to Jesus, his unwillingness to deny his faith, and his fourteen years of imprisonment and the horrific tortures that he faced as a result.

I remember longing to have what he had. I knew I did *not* want the imprisonment and tortures he had faced, but I wanted the sparkling treasure that emanated from *inside* of the man. He had something, to be honest, I didn't even know existed. He had the ability to view what I would have termed a living hell as the sweetest of blessings. He even referred to those who tortured him as "ones that he learned to love." I could not doubt the fact that what radiated out of him was a treasure gained through tremendous suffering.

After he concluded and the television screen went fuzzy, all of us just sat in silence, as if speaking would be irreverent. After a few minutes passed, Marky turned my way and smiled with an "I told you so" look all over his face. I whispered the only words that came into my head..."Wow!"

Afterwards, I could not get this precious man out of my mind. I longed for what he had more than I had ever wanted anything else in my life. This man understood the God of the Universe in the same way the apostle Andrew had, when he so willingly died for Him. It was real, it was tangible, it was alive *today* and not just buried in a history book.

What I witnessed was indomitable joy, unquenchable love, and mind-boggling peace. But I realized that it came with a price.

It was the "sweeter song" this aged man was singing! It's almost as if he was handing me the sheet music. I desperately wanted it; I wanted it played in my heart and in my life—I just didn't know if I wanted to pay the price to get it.

This old Romanian man was willing to give up everything, including his very life, to hear just a few sumptuous strains of that "sweeter song." What was *I* willing to give up?

When I was nineteen and a freshman in college, my ship had a head-on collision with God's ship. And for those of your who don't know, when you crash into the Living God, the encounter is certain to renovate every square inch of your life's boat.

Wimpy Christianity Exposed

I didn't even see the head-on collision coming. I actually thought things were going pretty well. Good grades, good table manners...I even had good hygiene! What else could possibly matter?

Okay, I'll admit I did have a little bit of an attitude problem. When I was fifteen I had been taught by my best friend, Blake, how to strut.

"No! No!" Blake had told me. "Do the chin bob, the eye squint, the snarl, and the swagger all at the *same* time! Not one after the other!"

I didn't learn it overnight, but by the age of nineteen, I had it down to a science.

"My name's Ludy!" I would boom in the bassiest, coolest sounding voice I could muster, *"Eric Ludy!"* I use to imagine that James Bond music continuously played in the background of my life.

To see me now, you may not believe this, but I use to be cool! *Really cool!*

Oh, I was a Christian! Don't get me wrong! It's just that my version of Christianity required never letting anyone know it. I even had good morals. I didn't drink (I'd had only a

couple swigs), I didn't smoke, I didn't cuss, and I was still...
(ahem) a virgin! Now there wasn't a soul alive whom I would
have told that "virgin" thing to when I was nineteen, so count
yourself privileged. Let's be honest here. Being a male capable of grunting, sweating, and not asking for directions, *but
not yet having conquered a woman*...in our culture, that
wasn't manhood, that was Dorksville!

Jesus Christ to me was nothing more than fire insurance.
I had found out when I was five what I needed to do to make
sure I didn't end up in hell. Like most people I know, I didn't
want to end up *there!*

"You need to *believe* Eric!" every Christian in my life had
told me. "*Believe* that Christ paid the price for your sins upon
the cross. Eric, He suffered and died in your place."

So little Eric, dressed in his favorite marmalade-orange
Winnie the Pooh jammies with red Popsicle stain all around
his tiny mouth, pronounced that he *beweeved.*

I *believed!* I *believed* that two thousand years ago, this
guy named Jesus was nailed to a tree. And that He took all my
sin upon himself, and that I can now know for certain I won't
end up in hell. I *believed* it, okay?

But then, if that's all there was to Christianity, why was
my life really no different than anyone else's who had good
morals, grades, manners, and hygiene?

Well, collide with God and you'll find out why. I had never
realized that there was more to Christianity than just believing.
There was something electrifyingly beautiful that I had never
known. I was on the brink of discovering the "sweeter song."

That Crazy Book!

I was reading a book when God's ship crashed into mine.
It was a book my sister, Krissy, had given me for Christmas
when I was a freshman in college.

"A book?" I had stated with wonder and great perplexity.
"It's a *book?*"

Those are the words my family heard. On the inside of my head it was, "A dumb book? It's a stinkin' *book?*"

My sister was famous for giving me great gifts. A Nerf ball when I was eleven, a muscle shirt and some weight gain powder when I was sixteen. Some of my favorite gifts had come from my sister. And now this? A stupid book.

"I think you're going to like it!" was all she said.

That "stinkin' book" haunted me for over a month, screaming at me from my bookshelf, "Read me! Are you illiterate or something?"

I'll never regret the moment I took that book from the shelf and opened it. My life has never since been the same. It was about a man in search of Truth. He looked everywhere! Eastern religions, various cults, and eventually biblical Christianity. And he found it! He found it in Jesus Christ!

I remember thinking, "Well, *I* know Jesus Christ!"

Not like this guy did! He recognized that Jesus had given *everything* for him, and the *least* he could do in return is give *everything* back to Jesus.

I had never in my life given *anything* to Jesus. The God of the Universe poured out His life for me, and I never once even considered what my response should be in the face of the most awesome sacrifice in the history of the world.

On my knees, I cried that evening. And I told the Creator of my life, the Lover of my soul, that He had unlimited access to the life of Eric Winston Ludy.

In a sense God boarded my ship. It was the ship that *I* had *always* captained, and now there was a little "king of the hill" dilemma. *I* had always called the shots, charted the course, chosen when to scrub the deck and what detergent to use. I mean, the ship had *my* name on the front! This had always been *my* ship!

In His ever gentle way, He moved into the Captain's Quarters.

I remember telling Him something similar to, "Okay! Make yourself comfortable. Re-carpet, re-wallpaper, do whatever You want in here. Uh, I'll just be down on the lower deck in *my* rooms."

For those of you who don't know, Christianity, if it were to be defined in very simplistic terms, would be: Me moving *out*, God moving *in*. Or you could look at it the way God made it clear to me...

Eric, are you ready to trust Me at the helm now? If I am Captain, we are going to have to make some changes. And Eric, the changes are going to have to be made to more than just the Captain's Quarters.

Protecting My Ludy Pride

"Clank, Clank!" He was knocking! I had rushed down into *my* rooms on the lower deck and had locked the doors. I didn't know quite what He meant by "more than just the Captain's Quarters."

What I had to realize is that when Jesus Christ takes over a life, He doesn't just want the helm and the hallways, He (gulp) wants the *entire ship!*

"Clank, Clank!" He kept knocking. The first room He was after was a room I felt He had no business tinkering with. "Clank, Clank!" As He continued to knock, I asked myself why God would even be interested in such a messy and smelly room. On the outside of the door I had a sign that read "Ludy Pride." Inside this room I had the "strut" that Blake taught me, my deep bassy voice, my "cool" attitude, even my moussed hairdo.

If God got ahold of this room, I knew it was Dorksville for me. If He stripped me of all these ingredients to "coolness," all that would be left would be...who I *really* was! And that was a scary thought!

"God!" I remember arguing, "If You come into this room, then I'm going to end up looking like an idiot!"

Then I had a stroke of genius!

"God! Someone may see me looking like an idiot...someone who knows I'm *also* a Christian. You wouldn't want that to happen! That might give *You* a bad name!"

Have you ever noticed that God *never* loses a debate?

God made it clear to me in His ever-gentle way that if He were concerned about His reputation, He would not have chosen someone like *me* to represent Him in the first place. And if He were pursuing popularity, he would not have allowed Himself to be hung naked between two thieves on a cross.

Eric! He was saying, *Your weakness is the soil in which I've chosen My strength and power to bloom in your life* (2 Corinthians 12:10 paraphrase).

The Clank, Clanks Continue

"Clank, Clank!" It seemed as soon as I opened one door, He would begin knocking on another. "Clank, Clank!"

"God! I know You're out there, " I said from behind deadbolted door number two, "but I just gave You my precious Ludy pride. Couldn't You go knock on someone else's door for a change?"

"Clank, Clank!"

Room number two was painted orange and blue with a life-size poster of John Elway on the wall. I would come to this room to eat corn chips and scream. On the door of this room hung a sign that read, "Beware: Rabid Bronco-Maniac Inside!" For some reason God wanted in!

"Clank, Clank!"

I use to dream in orange and blue (Bronco colors). The Denver Broncos were what I lived for. And more than a few times in the past twenty years, they were what I died for, too (Just check your handy Sports Almanac for details).

Eric! God was saying, *if you put your trust in mere men, they will let you down, but if you put your total trust in Me, I will NEVER let you down!*

As my mom put it when I was growing up,

"Eric, dear? If you cheer so loudly for the Denver Broncos, don't you think, Hon, that you should be cheering even louder for Jesus!"

That statement didn't go over very well with me when I was sixteen and obnoxiously chanting, "El-Way! El-Way!" But something was changing inside of me, and for the first time I was recognizing that Jesus *was* worthier of my cheers than John, and *He* deserved first place in my heart.

Not This Room!

"Clank, Clank!"

"No way!" I blared from behind door number three while installing an extra dead-bolt. "God, I have just given you my reputation and my Broncos; you have no business knocking on *this* door!"

"Clank, Clank!"

"God! You can have anything else; just please leave this room for me!" I pleaded.

"Clank, Clank!"

On the outside of the door to this room hung a sign that read, "Relationships With the Opposite Sex."

If there is one thing in all of life that we feel sure God has no clue about, it's romance. And you were not going to find me being the idiot who trusted God with my love life and ended up a Robinson Crusoe type of guy with a long white beard and shipwrecked on the desert island of singleness. Oh, no! And I also knew that if God did not grant me singleness, He would do something *even worse*. He would place forever at my side...THE BEAST!

I'd been to church! There are some funny looking people who sit in those pews. And if God loved *them,* then maybe He was going to call me to love one of them *too!*

"Clank, Clank!"

I know what you are thinking,

"ERIC, DON'T LET HIM IN!"

Because, you know that if *I* let Him in, you might feel convicted to consider letting Him into this room in *your* life, too. To be honest, I really struggled with this one. Not that I didn't struggle with my room of "Ludy Pride" and my prized "Bronco-Maniac" pad, but this was different. This room was not just a piece of my life, this room *was* my life. I mean, there was not much left to Eric Ludy if you took away what was in this room.

Weeks passed with a "Clank, Clank!" at the door, night and day. I remember asking myself, *"Why, Eric, can't you trust Him?"* I finally realized that my lack of trust came directly back to the fact that I didn't truly *know* Him.

If I could have taken just a little peek into God's father-heart—I mean just a *little* peek—I would have seen how much He delighted over me, how much He cherished and adored me! If I could have realized how interested He was in my highest good, I would have flung the door wide open.

I struggled with trusting Him, because I didn't truly know His nature and character. He created me; He knows me even better than I know myself. Why wouldn't I say to Him, "Not just *this* room, but Lord, I also want You to come into my other ten rooms down the hall!"

If you are longing for something more than the hit-and-run relationship cycle, something beautiful and meaningful in your life, then I'm going to lay it on the line. You must let go of the Captain's position in your life and trust Him. You must give up the little you're hanging on to now to gain something infinitely greater. You must let go of the helm and allow *Him* to lead.

After many weeks I unlocked the door. It was the single most risky thing I ever did in my life. I remember telling God, upon my knees with tears brimming in my eyes,

"I'm going to trust that You know what You are doing!"

Then, with a trembling heart, I made a commitment to my Captain.

"I'm willing for You to do whatever You want in this area of my life!" I swallowed hard, then continued, "I am willing, Almighty God, to be *single!* And Lord, if you desire me to someday get married, then the next girl I date and give my heart to will be the one *You show me* is my wife!"

Wounded for Heaven's Sake

Jesus once said to those closest to Him,

> *You're blessed when you are out of options, and all you can do is lean on God. Because when you realize your need for God, it is only then that you tap into His immeasurable greatness and goodness.*
>
> *You're blessed when you've been stripped of that which is most precious to you. Because only then can you be tenderly embraced by the One most precious to you.*
>
> Matthew 5:3-5 (paraphrase)

Jesus originally spoke those words in Greek. And the Greek meaning of the word blessed is "supreme happiness."

Jesus Himself gave us the key to unlocking the treasure chest where the sheet music to the "sweeter song" is held. Remember how I said earlier that there is something better out there when it comes to love, but it is found in a very unexpected place? Well, the unexpected place is *God Himself.* And to find the "something better" we have to "lean on God" and be "stripped of that which is most precious to us." In a sense, we have to be willing to become vulnerable to *trust* Him if we wish to find security and satisfaction *in* Him. We have to be willing let go of what little we have, to gain the great riches and supreme happiness He has to offer. And we have to let Him have the helm if we wish to hear the "sweeter song."

The "something better" is found in emptying yourself, surrendering to His lead, letting go of your life and all you hold dear, and entrusting *everything* to Him. Because in doing that, you will be tenderly embraced by the sweetest Musician in all the Universe and receive your own personal concert.

Letting go is not easy for any of us. But Jesus makes it very clear that to go where He is going and to be a part of His wondrous plan we must,

"...deny ourselves, pick up our cross daily, and follow Him" (Luke 9:23 paraphrase).

A more rude translation might be,

"If you are truly serious about being a follower of Me, then each and every day you are going to need to die to *your* way of doing things, trust Me at the helm, and allow me to Captain your ship! Oh, and Eric? That means I can take your ship wherever I see fit! Trust Me, I love you more than you could ever comprehend, and I have your very best in mind!"

One of my heroes is a man named Jim Elliot. He was a man who not only inspired me in my love story with Leslie, but he inspired me with his abandonment to his Captain, Jesus Christ. I read his words years after his amazing and sacrificial death at the hands of the Auca Indians whom he was attempting to reach with the Gospel. He simply said:

> *He is no fool who gives what he cannot keep to gain what he cannot lose.*[2]

To discover life, Jesus says you have to give yours up (Luke 9:24; John 12:25). Your love life is no different. If you really desire to one day discover the "beautiful side of love" you have to first walk through the "painful side." Just like pouring concrete is not the exciting part of building a house yet the *essential* part, the same is true with building a magnificent romance. Laying your life down is not the fun and enjoyable part; it's the *essential* part!

If God is going to write your love story, He's going to first need your pen. If God is going to lead your love boat to the harbor of romance beyond the fairy-tales, He needs the helm. As Jesus once said to his followers:

> *Daily you must trust Me, surrendering everything, including the blood in your veins and the breath in your lungs, for Me to do with as I see fit. If you want to join up with Me, you must let Me lead.*
> Luke 9:23 (paraphrase)

If ever you are going to hear the "sweeter song" that God created you to hear, then you're going to have to first open the door to Jesus and let Him have *His* way. And you are going to have to trust that He, as the inventor of romance, knows how to write a beautiful tale!

> *The floods washed away home and mill, all the poor man had in the world. But as he stood on the scene of his loss, after the water had subsided, brokenhearted and discouraged, he saw something shining in the bank which the waters had washed bare. "It looks like gold," he said. It was gold. The flood which had beggared him made him rich.*[3]
> Henry Clay Trumbull

A Step Further

Many thousands of years ago three young men willingly surrendered their lives to God, and a nation was changed because of it. Crack your Bible open to Daniel chapter 3 and read about it! Then grab yourself a pen and a sheet of paper and prayerfully write down the areas that you need to let go of in your own life.

Chapter Four

Leslie:
Rubbing Shoulders with
the Author of Romance

Following a faithful Father,
not a faulty formula

Meeting Eric's First Girlfriend

I should have known I was in for a ride the moment I found out from a Japanese foreign exchange student that, "In Japan, 'Ludy' mean nerd!"

I had always hoped that the man I married would have a nice conservative last name, like Smith or Jones. But it was not to be. Ludy is *not* a "normal" last name (Japan is now off-limits to us unless we go incognito). And Eric Ludy, who I affectionately call "Beef" (it's a long story, okay?) is certainly not a "normal" character—how can he be with a name like *that?* As you may have guessed, our adventure together so far has been anything but "normal!" To put it bluntly, I married a man who collects embarrassing moments. Being his wife, I get to share in the humiliation right along with him!

After five months of wedded bliss, I remember standing in the kitchen while overhearing a phone conversation between Eric and a "big wig" at a major university's medical school department. Eric was planning to become a doctor, and he was discussing program requirements with the head professor.

"Okay," I heard Eric reply, "you just need my name and address and you can send it? Great. It's Eric Ludy. Uh, huh. That's L-O-O-D-Y."

Panic gripped me as I realized Eric had just misspelled his own last name for one of his future med. school professors.

"No!" I screeched in the background. (I couldn't think of anything else to say!)

Just when my cry reached his ears, Eric realized his blunder and quickly corrected his statement.

So what the prof. heard was, "Eric Ludy. That's L-O-O-D-Y...uh wait, no, I mean actually it's L-U-D-Y!"

Course requirement number one—know how to spell your own last name! Needless to say, Eric *didn't* go to medical school. You never know when or how those defining moments in your career will happen.

Instead of med. school, we went into ministry—challenging our generation to entrust their love lives to God. Some people think that from the time I was five years old, this was my life-long dream. Uh...no. It wasn't. In fact, one of our first speaking engagements was to a large gathering of youth. I looked out at the audience full of grungy, shaggy teens with their baggy pants and scruffy goatees and almost fled through the back door.

"God," I remember thinking, "I paid my dues as a teenager already! I think going through adolescence *once* was enough punishment! Why do You have to take me right back into this den of hormone-crazed humanity?"

I could just picture getting up in front of this crowd of kids—who were either slumped in their seats with their arms crossed, or entangled with a member of the opposite sex— and telling them, *"Hey people! Give your love life to God! Doesn't that sound great?!"*

Yeah, right.

Well, somehow, miraculously, we made it through that night alive (it must have been those bulletproof vests we were wearing).

But to my surprise, the audience listened. They even responded to the message! And thus began our unforgettable journey to share the "beautiful side of love" with our love-hungry generation.

Being a public speaker AND married to an avid collector of embarrassing moments is an interesting combination. Everyone watches you all the time. *"Ooooh, look at her. She's going into the bathroom! Wow! Let's go see what she's doing in there!"* Believe me, that has actually happened…more than once.

At one event, Eric told the group that he used to *kiss his pillow* when he was a teenager! Now wait a minute! If he wants to subject himself to everyone and their dog knowing his deepest secrets, that's his business. The only problem is when you're married, his business *is* your business! I might as well have kissed my pillow, too!

Of course, *they loved* the revelation. Any dirt you can get on the speaker is gold.

The next morning we were invited to speak at the Sunday morning service. I had forgiven him for the pillow-kissing thing and it was all in the past. Eric was waiting for an introduction from the pastor before he approached the podium, so in the meantime he was going over his notes, reviewing some of his key points. Neither of us was expecting the "shock of the century."

The pastor at the podium looked down at us with a loving smile breaking across his devious face, then announced,

"We so appreciated Eric and Leslie and the message God has given them."

Eric and I looked at each other and smiled.

The pastor continued, "And just to show our appreciation, we have a surprise for them. Last night on the late night flight from Denver, we were able to locate, and fly in, Eric's *first* girlfriend!"

"WHAT?! ERIC'S FIRST GIRLFRIEND? How disgusting! I don't want to meet *her*! These people are such jerks!" I screamed to myself inside my head with a huge smile plastered over my face.

Beside me Eric had dropped his notes and had a coronary. He couldn't even remember who his first girlfriend *was*! But his face, in perfect speaker style, reflected a joyful calm.

The pastor kept us in suspense a few more minutes, then finally said, "We'd like for you all to meet Eric's first girlfriend. Please give her a warm welcome."

Then, as we held our breath, he reached behind the podium and pulled out for all to see...*a pillow*. The audience howled. And to this day the pillow-kissing jokes have not subsided. In fact, we even have a huge mail-bin at home entitled "Pillow-Kisser's Anonymous Club Correspondence." Great idea, Eric, to tell that little story. It will haunt us for the rest of our lives!

Yes, there are some pitfalls to what we do; the pillow-kissing jokes, the curiosity-struck onlookers following me into the bathroom, and the strange animosity I have developed towards Eric's first girlfriend (I'm still working on curbing my jealousy). But in spite of all this, I really *have* enjoyed our anything-but-normal-journey. And there's a reason I put up with all the embarrassing moments just to share this vitally important message with my generation—not too long ago, *my* life was changed forever by its simple truth...

My Not-So-Perfect Plan

As a Christian young woman navigating my way through the murky waters of the dating scene, I used to believe that God didn't have much interest in my love life other than to make sure I wasn't "going too far." I had been boy-crazy from the age of about seven, and so from an early age my parents had made sure I was well versed on the "Christian" way of dating. Years before, I was officially allowed to begin my "dating career." I had memorized the "two rules of Christian dating":

Rule #1: Don't have sex until marriage

Rule #2: Make sure you date only people who share your beliefs and values

Somehow I perceived that as long as I obeyed these two "Christian dating rules" I could pretty much make my own decisions when it came to issues like who to date, when to date, how to date, even who to get serious about. I truly desired to obey God and do things "the right way" in this area of my life. Yet in the back of my mind, I was determined to create just as much excitement as possible in my upcoming love life without compromising my Christian standards. I didn't think it would be hard. Before I even started high school, I had developed a brilliant plan for how things were going to work over the next few years.

"I can't wait to start dating!" I would tell my friends at slumber parties. "I'm just going to date around for fun during high school and college, go to all the dances and parties and football games, and have a ton of different boyfriends."

Don't get me wrong, I *did* believe that someday I would meet the "right guy" and that we would ride off into the sunset to live happily ever after. But as far as I was concerned, that was *years* away. It wouldn't happen until I was older and life had lost a little of its zest. And besides, I was sure that I would forget every relationship I'd ever had once my husband came into my life. In the meantime, having fun was all that mattered.

So with great excitement, I eagerly plunged into one temporary relationship after another, striving to maintain "a ton of different boyfriends" and going to all the dances, parties, and football games.

As the years went by, I realized that my innocent childhood dreams were not to be. My life was full of emptiness. On the outside it looked as though I was a solid, confident Christian young woman, conducting my love life in a mature and godly way. Yet all was not as it seemed. Where I once had put my hope and confidence in my relationship with Christ, I now began to cling desperately to each relationship that came into my life in order to find my security and purpose. My dating life became my identity. My emotions became hopelessly entangled in each rocky relationship. The cutting, brutal pain of ending a relationship, no matter how serious or shallow it had been, drove me to constantly lower my "Christian" standards and bend the rules as much as possible, so as to somehow hold onto each guy who came into my life. But it never worked. I compromised myself to the point where I was ridden with guilt and overcome with depression.

I had dreamed of a perfect fairy-tale love story someday. I had pictured a blissful and carefree dating life, just like what I watched on the black and white TV shows. But I hadn't known about the "ugly" side of the temporary dating cycle…the inevitable heartbreak, confusion, and compromise of my spiritual values.

I remember keeping a death-grip on my relationship with Travis, the popular, athletic basketball player whom I had managed to snag after meeting him at a game. Our casual, flirtatious friendship soon turned into a serious, passionate romance. I always felt so secure when Travis put his arm gently on my shoulder as we entered a crowded room full of strangers.

The relationship went strong for about eight months, but then he started waking up to the fact that there were other girls who were interested in him. Not only that, these other young women were willing to have sex with him. Still attempting to follow the Christian dating rule #1, I had told Travis that I couldn't go "all the way" with him. At first, he had accepted this condition readily. He even said that as a Christian himself, he agreed with my commitment to abstinence until marriage. But there came a point where I noticed his interested gaze resting upon other girls who looked at him seductively with open invitation. I could sense the end of our relationship coming. In desperation, I lowered my standards in the area of purity as much as I felt I possible could, giving Travis as many "physical favors" as I dared. But it was no use. Soon it was over and he was giving his love and devotion to someone else, pretending he didn't even know who I was anymore. We had shared everything for almost a year of our lives, and now we were strangers.

This was the constant pattern of my love life. Each fling ended with heartbreak and shattered emotions. Each time, I felt used and defiled. The perfect plan I had so carefully crafted for my dating career was crumbling. Before I had even graduated from high school, I literally felt like I had been through the turmoil of about five major divorces. I had no more confidence. I didn't know who I was anymore, and I really didn't even care.

Giving God the Pen

Tell God you are ready to be offered, and God will prove Himself to be all you ever dreamed He would be.[1]

Oswald Chambers

Finally, I could handle it no longer. Sobbing my eyes out in misery, I cried out to God, "Why is this happening to me? I am living a moral life, following Your commands, yet I am miserable! Why aren't You blessing this area of my life? I'm still following the Christian rules—but I'm so unhappy. I'm doing the best I can, and I'm still making a mess of things! If I keep going at this rate, I'll be an official basket-case before I'm twenty!"

In a soft, tender way I felt a tugging on my heart. God was trying to get my attention, to open my eyes to a truth that would change my life. If that moment could have been translated into a conversation with God, it would have sounded something like this:

> *Leslie, don't you believe that I know who you will marry, and that I'm capable of leading you to that right man someday?*

"Of course, I believe that, God, but what does that have to do with the here and now?"

> *Well, Leslie, can you also believe that I am the God of all creation? I know you better than you know yourself, and I am perfectly able to bring this man into your life in My own time, in My own way...and I don't need your help.*

For the first time I realized that God had more of an interest in my love life than just making sure I followed a few rules. He wanted to be *involved!* And, more than that, He wanted to write my love story for me...*without my help!*

A mixture of emotions came with that realization. First, I felt instant doubt and fear. Could God really do this without *my* help? Even though I had messed up my love life so far, I was pretty sure I still had *way more* insight into the finer things in life like love, sex, dating, and marriage, than someone as old (and most likely out-dated) as *God!* What if He butchered the whole thing? I pictured myself trusting God with this precious area of my life, only to end up sitting in a long, gray tent-like dress, staring forlornly out the window and rocking my life away. No friends, no phone calls, no life whatsoever. I wouldn't get married until I was ninety-three, and it would be to some Elmer Fudd type of guy I couldn't stand. We'd have four horrible years together, then die.

Looking back, I laugh at such a thought. That was before I learned what a "romantic" God is! If I had only known what He had planned for me...I never would have doubted for a minute!

The second emotion I felt was relief. I had been trying to make sense out of this area of my life for so long, and I had had the pressure of figuring everything out for myself. *What if I marry the wrong person? What if I never meet the right guy? How will I know who the right one is? What if I make a mistake and ruin my whole life?* Constant worries like these had been my companions for years. Now God was giving me an invitation to give all of these fears to Him—and to let Him lead and guide me through each step. I didn't have to carry the weight anymore; I could lay it completely in His hands! What freedom! But was it too good to be true? Could I *really* trust Him?

That day, I felt His challenge to me...could I trust Him enough to lay it all in His hands? Would He really take an active role in this area of my life? Would He lead and guide? And of even more concern to me was the question, would He lead me where I did *not* want to go? (The rocking chair-Elmer Fudd scenario gave me nightmares!)

I went through several days of intense inward struggle. While the Christian world indicated that I was following God's way by keeping the rules as best as possible, deep down I knew I was really the one in control of this area of my life. I had been the one calling the shots, not God.

Letting go of this area of my life seemed impossible. And yet a soft whisper to my heart reminded me that if I was ever going to be truly happy or fulfilled, and if I was ever going to stop making such a mess of things, *He* had to be in the center. Trusting Him completely with my love life was probably the hardest decision I had ever faced.

Finally, I surrendered to the gentle inward tug upon my heart. I knelt beside my bed and prayed, *"Lord, this is such a hard area to give to You. I desperately want to hold on to it, and do things my way. Yet, I know You are asking me to lay it in Your hands, to let You take charge of it. So, now, I give it to You. No matter what You choose to do with this area of my life, even if it's something I never would have chosen for myself, I give it to You. Do with me what You will. I am Yours."*

My God-written love story began at that moment. God took the pen from my trembling hand and began scripting the most incredible tale imaginable. No, my future husband did not show up at my front door right then. But from that day on, God began healing and restoring the pain of my mistakes and molding and preparing me for *true* love. Before Eric came into my life, God had a few foundation stones to lay in place.

Priority Check

The reason some of us are such poor specimens of Christianity is because we have no Almighty Christ. We have Christian attributes and experiences, but there is no abandonment to Jesus Christ.[2]

Oswald Chambers

So, I had given God the pen to write my love story. But, practically, what did that mean for me on a daily basis? I was in the height of my "dating career" and not planning on marriage anytime soon. Was I supposed to stop dating? Were friendships with guys okay? How would I know when God *wanted* me to get into a relationship? When knowing adults asked me that infamous question, "So, Leslie, is there any special guy in your life right now?" what was I supposed to say? What did God want me to do?

During the weeks and months after my decision to allow God to be in control of this area of my life, another gentle message was being communicated to my heart by His still, small whisper. It went something like,

Leslie, don't try to build Me into your life anymore... instead, build your life around Me. It was true. I had tried to "fit God into my life" by praying each morning, reading my Bible every night, and attending church weekly. Yet He was not the central focus of my daily life. In reality I was only giving Him a few minutes of scattered attention here and there. I finally came to the realization that unless I slowed down and made a genuine effort to *seek Him* instead of just being so consumed with my own ambitions, I would have a hard time discerning His will for me in *any* area.

So I embarked upon a journey to get to know my Creator. And truthfully, I wasn't sure what was going to happen. I mean, I had gone from revolving my life around a whirlwind of social activities, friends, and dating relationships, to saying, "Lord, I'm going to lay all that aside and focus on You instead." Not that those other things were necessarily wrong, but God was asking me to put my priorities straight. My dating and social life had become so distracting that I could no longer hear His voice clearly.

As Elisabeth Elliot says in her book *A Chance to Die* (about the life of Amy Carmichael), "The preoccupations of seventeen-year-old girls—their looks, their clothes, their social life—don't change much from generation to generation. But, in every generation there seem to be a few who make other choices. Amy Carmichael was one of the few."[3]

And God was calling me to be one of those "few" as well. But I didn't know how.

"If You want this for me Lord, You are going to have to help me," I silently told Him.

And He did! He met me right where I was and taught me about Himself. I learned how to love Him with my whole heart, to seek Him earnestly, to listen to His voice on a daily basis, and to fall in love with His Word. It was the most exciting time of my life! It made the world of social frenzy I had come from seem incredibly empty. Daily I discovered more about who He is, and more about who He wanted me to become. I started a journal—and have kept it up to this very day—in which I wrote prayers, fears, and desires to the Lord. I also recorded anything I felt He might be teaching me, be it through Scripture or a gentle pull upon my heart. Now when I look back at my old entries, I am amazed at how faithful He was to put every detail of my life in place at the perfect time.

Yes, I lost some friends (but in reality they weren't real friends anyway). And yes, I lost popularity. Yet what I gained was priceless...Jesus Christ as my first love, my very Best Friend.

It may not seem that this part of my story has much to do with my relationship with Eric. *But it was the whole key.* There are two reasons why letting Christ into this place in my life was the foundation of my love story with Eric.

1. I learned to lean on my relationship with Christ for my hope, joy, and security, rather than trying to find those things in a romantic relationship. As close to Prince Charming as Eric is, he still is only human (a fact which I still have to remind him of from time to time)! If I had gone into my relationship with him looking for all my emotional needs to be met, I would have been disappointed. I wasn't truly ready to begin a journey toward marriage with my future husband until I learned to find my hope and security in Christ alone.

2. Jesus Christ remained at the center of my relationship with Eric. Jesus Christ was the passion of my heart when I met Eric Ludy. Jesus Christ was the passion of Eric's heart as well. As a result, we were drawn together in friendship because of our mutual love for the Lord. The more time we spent together, the more we grew closer to God through each other. Whenever I discovered a new truth in the Word of God, I couldn't wait to share it with Eric. We spent hours talking about our Lord and our faith. When we started to have deeper feelings than friendship for each other, God guided us each and every step as we began moving into a romantic relationship. He remained at the center.

Sometimes in a relationship, we can be so caught up in our feelings for the other person that we squeeze God into the background. It becomes a confusing, emotional mess, and we wonder why God isn't giving us more direction, when all the while He is there, waiting to be allowed back into first place in our hearts. Only when He is truly in first place are we ready for a God-written love story.

It's Not About a Formula

Even after we place our love life into the hands of God, it is so easy to revert to looking for a "magic formula" to figure everything out. I cannot count the number of times I get asked questions like, *"Is it wrong for me to date?"* or *"What do you do when you think you've met the right one?"* To which I must reply...ask *Him!*

People often get frustrated and say, "Well, I asked Him and He isn't giving any answers!"

Jana, a bubbly first year student at a university in California, made the decision to give God the pen of her love story nearly two years ago. The problem is, since then Jana hasn't received any direction for this area of her life, and she is aggravated at God.

"I just don't get it," she complains. "When I gave this area to God, I expected Him to bring Prince Charming across my path. But every relationship I have gotten into has *still* turned out all wrong. Why isn't God getting involved? Why hasn't He done anything miraculous in this area of my life?"

As I look at Jana's daily life, I realize that although she attempted to give God control, she never re-oriented her lifestyle to revolve around her relationship with Him. She expects answers from God without pursuing Him at all. Her idea of "seeking Him" is a once-a-week, five-minute Bible reading where she opens His Word randomly and reads whatever Scripture her eyes fall upon. No flash of divine wisdom comes, so she goes on her merry way, convinced that if God wants to speak to her, He'll have to send a heavenly messenger or a bolt of lightening to point her in the right direction.

Inviting God to write the chapters of our love story involves work on our part—not just a scattered prayer here and there, not merely a feeble attempt to find some insight by flopping open the Bible every now and then. It's seeking Him on a daily basis, putting Him in first place at all times, discovering His heart.

He may not come down with a bolt of lightening or paint a message for you in the sky, but as you truly get to know Him and His Word, you will understand His desires for you. It takes effort. It isn't easy. But it's the key to discovering the "sweeter song."

Wouldn't it be nice if we could write a book called, *Ten Steps For Achieving a Perfect Love Story,* and give you a foolproof, cookie-cutter blueprint for how it's all supposed to work?

But God cares too much about us to give us a formula. He wants us to lean on Him for guidance and direction. He wants to be intimately involved in each detail, in every step of the way. The minute we try to rely on a formula, we miss out on the whole beauty of what a God-written love story is all about. Eric and I have met plenty of people who are desperately trying to "get it right" by following a set of rules for a godly relationship. And they are usually miserable, frustrated, and depressed with the whole attempt.

Don't get me wrong; there are clear and unquestionable commands God gives us in Scripture for this area of our lives, such as sexual purity before marriage, avoiding marriage to an unbeliever, absolute faithfulness after marriage, etc. These are guidelines from a loving and faithful Father, because He wants the very best for us.

But there *are* a few "gray areas" that can leave us thoroughly confused. The variety of opinion among Christians in this area of relationships is endless.

There is the camp that casually declares (in surfer lingo, of course), "Dude, just try not to have sex before marriage, and if you accidentally do, that's a bummer, but hey, we all mess up, you know? All you have to do is, like, ask for forgiveness and everything's cool."

Then there is the group that firmly says (in a fiery, down-home twang), "No talkin' to the opposite sex, no sir! Don't even lay eyes on 'em! Ya better flee that evil temptation before ya burn in hell!"

And of course there is every teaching in between these two extremes. The problem is that no matter what side of the pendulum swing we are on, either just doing the bare minimum requirement or going to ultra-strict extremes...if we are trying to follow a "rule" just because we have to, inside we become resentful and begrudging. We aren't obeying commands because we love God and want to please Him; we are doing it simply because it's expected of us.

Rules, Rules, Rules!

Trying to build a foolproof formula for a godly relationship can only end in failure. Whenever we put our trust in rules to protect us, we push God out of first place in our lives.

I grew up with the "Dude-just-try-not-to-have-sex" mentality, thinking that as long as I gave it a shot and attempted to stay within certain boundaries, (i.e., abstinence before marriage) this area of my life would be protected from harm. However, the boundaries I created for myself still gave me plenty of room to compromise without technically "overstepping" them. Even though I was still within the fences I put up, I was living a life of heartache and despair.

Sarah, a pretty blonde with a knack for the melodramatic, had an experience on the other extreme. She came from a church with excessively strict and specific rules about guy-girl relationships. As she puts it, "There were so many rules to follow, you had to keep a list taped to your bathroom mirror just to remember them all!"

Sarah met John, the resident "godly heart-throb-with-cute-curls" at church, and eventually they felt God leading them toward marriage. They followed every rule down to the last letter. From the outside, it would appear as if there was no way they could fall into any sort of compromise with such strict supervision and guidelines. They were never allowed to be alone together; they weren't even permitted to have any sort of physical contact, and their parents were intricately involved in every decision about their relationship.

Sarah recalls, "We were so confident that we were following the right path, we thought we were immune to sin."

But rules did not save them from temptation, and one day Sarah and John found themselves in sexual sin. She became pregnant, and they were forced to get married right away. They disappointed their families, their church, and themselves, but they learned a valuable lesson...no matter how many rules we make for ourselves, rules don't create a godly relationship. *Only leaning on our Faithful Father, and longing to please Him with everything we do will set the stage for a beautiful romance!*

Is it a Chore or a Choice?

In our abandonment we give ourselves over to God just as God gave Himself for us, without any calculation. The consequences of abandonment never enters into our outlook because our life is taken up with Him.[4]

Oswald Chambers

Do you remember as a child, being forced by your parents to submit to slave labor? You know, when they made you bear the heavy yoke of cleaning up the kitchen after dinner? If you were at all like me, you probably weren't too thrilled about doing the terrible task, and maybe you even complained the whole way through. My famous line was the tearful accusation, "You treat me just like Cinderella!" while dramatically leaning on the broom with a beaten and downtrodden look, as if I were going to faint from exhaustion. (My pathetic cry for mercy never seemed to move my parents to sympathy.)

But no matter how much you hated the awful chore, you did it anyway. Why? Because you knew that negative consequences would result if you did not. Your parents had already made terrible threats, like grounding you from your bike, or sending you to your room if you did not obey. Like me, you probably did the bare minimum requirement just to get the job done, and you constantly asked, "Can I be done yet?!" until they finally set you free from the dungeon of kitchen-torture!

Now try to recall another memory. We all had our angelic moments as children. For some like me, those moments were rare, but still they *did* exist. At one time or another, you probably experienced something similar to the following scenario.

Your parents went out for the evening. The kitchen was a mess, but no one asked you to clean it. You got the brilliant idea to do something "special" for Mom and Dad. So you set to work (all by yourself!) and scrubbed the dishes. You did an extra-careful job to get them sparkling clean. You even wiped up the counters and swept the floor. (Now that is *really* going the extra mile!) You couldn't wait for your parents to come home and notice what you had done. When they arrived and exclaimed, "Who cleaned up the kitchen?! This is wonderful!" your heart swelled with pride. Remember that feeling? You actually *enjoyed* the whole process. Cleaning the kitchen went from a dull drudgery to an act of joy. Why? Because you were not motivated by a rule, but by love for your parents.

When obeying God is a chore that we are "forced" to do, it becomes a lifeless act of drudgery and we complain the whole way through. God becomes the Big-No-Fun-One trying to make our lives miserable.

But when we learn who God *really* is and we base our decisions out of a passionate love for Him, we find joy and delight in obedience. We even *want* to go that extra mile for Him!

What It's Really All About

As Christians, we need a new mindset toward God's involvement in this area of our lives. Whether you grew up with the "just-try-not-to-have-premarital-sex" crowd, or you had a ten-page rulebook for relationships, either approach denies the beauty of God's ways.

Remember the infamous question that most of us learned back in the days of youth group pow-wow sessions? That's right... *"How far is too far?"* (which is really a code question asking, "How much can I get away with and not make God mad?") Let's start asking a new question...

"How far can I possibly go to bring joy to the heart of my heavenly Father in this area of my life?"

Once you get to know your King in a personal way, once Jesus Christ becomes the focus and passion of your life, it's not hard at all to ask that question, because it flows from a heart of overwhelming love for your Lord. If you say genuinely, "How can I please you, Lord?" He will show you, each and every day, in His own gentle way. The answer won't be drudgery to which you are forced to comply. When you love Him, *really* love Him, you will be able to say with David the psalmist:

> *I delight to do Thy will, O my God.*
>
> Psalm 40:8 NIV

God has created us all as individuals, and He has a unique and special plan for each of our lives. *Don't settle for a formula.* If you're ready for an unforgettable romance, start by discovering the joy of an intimate, daily romance with the King of Kings. And let the adventure begin!

A Step Further

In ancient times, there was once a man who trusted God so much that he willingly gave up his most prized and treasured possession when God asked him for it. The amazing things that happened as a result were just plain miraculous! This story ranks in history as one of the greatest tales of love, surrender, and abandoning all to trust God that has ever been told! Turn to Genesis chapter 22 and read the story that has deeply impacted millions throughout the centuries. Allow God to gently hold your heart in His hands, and teach you how you can discover that deeper level of trust and abandonment in your own personal walk with Him.

Section Two

Preparing for a Love Story

Chapter Five

Eric:
Get a Love Life!

*Learning to love your
future spouse even before you meet*

What If I Get a Belly?

Love matures throughout a relationship, or at least it is supposed to. I remember getting jealous and overprotective of Leslie when a Kirk Cameron-look-alike took her order at Taco Bell. I also remember the insecurity I felt when a curly-headed hunk came to church and sat a couple of chairs down from her. I looked down at my own biceps (they were so small they both added up to only one) and winced. Immature love always compares and snivels and struggles with the security of the relationship.

Many relationships unfortunately never discover the liberty and the confidence found in a mature love life.

"Eric?" Leslie sheepishly asked me one day, "Who were the other girls who you use to date?"

"Les!" I awkwardly fidgeted, "I don't want to talk about *them!* Let's talk about *us!*"

It was a good six months before our wedding day and our less-than-mature love was battling with a serious case of the "single-with-a-low-self-esteem" blues.

"Were they beautiful?" she continued to probe.

"Uh!" I floundered, "Uh, no. No!" I gained confidence and trumpeted with a twinkle in my love struck eyes, "They were ugly!" (Note: Any previous girlfriends of mine who read this book, please don't hate me for saying that. I didn't have much of a choice.)

"What type of personalities did they have? What color hair? How tall were they? How wide were they?" Question after question came shooting my way.

Believe me! If you have never experienced a conversation like this, it is *hard. Really* hard! I solemnly refer to this legendary conversation as "the night my dirty laundry was exposed!"

With tears in my eyes, I shared with the young woman who I loved more than anyone in this world that I had not always cherished her. The way I had lived was solid proof. I told her, in as much detail as she and I could handle, how in the past I had carelessly *not* considered *her* needs and had sought to meet my own instead. We cried and hugged, and cried some more. For a pain-filled ten minutes we silently held each other as tears streamed down our cheeks and the knife of regret turned in my heart. Then, ever gently, she sat back and turned my chin so that I could see her wet eyes, and she spoke the sweetest, most healing words my ears have ever heard,

"Eric," her dainty little voice haltingly whispered, "I forgive you!"

With her hand she touched my cheek and with her trembling lips she said, "Eric, *I love you!* You are my hero, my prince charming, and my noble knight in shining armor! And I have chosen to love you just like my precious Jesus loves me!"

There are people in this world who think they "have it good." But they don't know what living is all about until they receive love like *that.* I did not deserve it, but the love-of-my-life chose to give it to me.

It is a humbling thing to receive that kind of unwarranted acceptance and embrace. Our culture teaches us to love *with condition.* We love as long as we "feel" love, we love as long as our lover meets our needs, and we love as long as they look lovely on the outside.

A few days after my "dirty laundry" night, I was dealing with another bout of the "single-with-low-self-esteem" blues. We had just visited an old buddy of Leslie's. He just happened to be male, macho, and multi-talented. All afternoon I compared myself to him, with insecure thoughts constantly bouncing through my head like a pinball on caffeine.

"Maybe he would be a better man for Leslie than me? Maybe she would enjoy him more than me? Maybe I am not good enough for someone so sweet and perfect as Leslie?"

As I said, immature love is great at comparing and sniveling. What I found, is that one of the greatest ways to grow up love to maturity is to personally receive it in its most extravagant and undiluted form.

I had just exposed my insecurity to Leslie and was staring at the floor with that whipped-dog expression.

"Eric?" Leslie giggled, "How could you even think that?"

I just shrugged my shoulders in response.

"Eric, you need to know that *I don't want anyone else.* I'm not even looking! I don't want to grow old with Dirk (Dirk-the-Dork is *my* affectionate name for him). I want to grow old with *you!*"

I grew up constantly scrutinizing my appearance, my hairdo, my complexion, my wardrobe, my strut, my bassy voice, even my personal fragrance. I tirelessly labored to maintain "the image of perfection" for risk of never being accepted by a beautiful young woman. I was afraid that if I didn't get as close as possible to the "Ken doll aura," I wouldn't ever be worthy of a woman's love.

Now here I was years later, totally realizing *my unworthiness* of a woman's love, yet accepted and loved by a woman. *Now* the question became, "Is it possible to lose her love if I lose what attracted her to me in the first place?"

"Even if you get a belly and go bald I'm going to love you, Eric! You can't lose my love, because it's *not* a love I need to feel—it is a love that I have chosen!"

Then she gave me a powerful illustration of what type of love she was choosing to have for me.

"Eric, even if you were in a horrible accident and you were stuck in a wheelchair the rest of your life and I couldn't even recognize the man I married in your disfigured face...I would love you just the same!"

Wow! (Do I have good taste or what?) And that is a kind of love that many humans throughout history have sought for and never found, because they searched in the wrong places.

Many of you are thinking, "I want to love like *that!* But, how can I until I have *my lover* in my life?"

Well, as strange as this might seem, you don't need to be married to love like *that*. It's critical that you note this *very* important fact—your love life is not supposed to kick into gear when you finally meet that future someone special. Oh, no! If you are a true romantic the way God created you to be, you need to put it in gear right here and now! In fact, go ahead and floor it! For all you singles who have been longing for a love life, I have wonderful news...*you have one!* The moment you meet the Great Lover of your soul is the very moment that you kick off your passionate love life!

Your Love Life

If we cut off their tongues and forbid the Christians speech, they love with their hands, with their feet, and with their eyes, they love always and everywhere until their last respiration. Does anybody know how to take out the power of love from these stupid Christians?[1]

Romanian prison guard who found both his fulfillment and frustration in torturing Christians

Love is the cologne of Christ. You can't get close to Him without catching its overwhelming fragrance. Love is the scent of Christ's true followers, too. And it's the fragrance of love that we, as Christ's followers, are personally responsible to drench ourselves in. Take off the cologne cap and just dump it. The heavier the aroma, the more of Jesus this world will understand and know.

Jesus wasn't mincing words when He said, *You will know my followers by their love.* In other words, if there is no scent of Christ's love on someone, then they bear no evidence of true devotion to Christ. Love is our badge as Christians. Just as an FBI agent whips out his ID and states, "FBI!" we as Christians whip out our attitudes, actions, and words to prove "I am with *Him!*"

Most people never realize that the way we live displays in vivid color, for all the world to see, everything from what we believe in to what we worship and bow down to. You can share a message without ever opening your mouth. Just listen to this story.

Love Can't Be Imprisoned!

In a cold dank prison cell lay a pastor who was bleeding, bruised, and torture-weary. It was a cell reserved for the dying. There were others in the "death cell," prisoners beaten and suffering, preparing to die. Iseu, the pastor, though his strength was gone, spoke to the others about the beauties of heaven and the love of Jesus. His body was still on earth, but mentally he was already in heaven.

One of the other prisoners was the Communist who had tortured Iseu to this point of death. The government had arrested their own comrade and tortured him. Now he, too, was near death.

The prisoner who witnessed the following drama described it as a scene from heaven saying, "You need not be in heaven to see heaven."

The despairing Communist awoke in the night and cried out, "Please, pastor, say a prayer for me. I have committed such crimes. I cannot die."

The agonizing pastor, leaning on two of the other prisoners for support, slowly made his way to the torturer's side. Iseu caressed his torturer on his head and said, "I have forgiven you with all of my heart and I love you. If I, who am only a sinner, can love and forgive you, more so can Jesus who is the Son of God and who is love incarnate. Return to Him. He longs for you much more than you wish to be forgiven. You just repent."

In the dark cell where hardness and hopelessness were the usual companions, the torturer found the most tender affection and the most unmerited mercy. The torturer confessed all his murders to the tortured one and they prayed together. Then the two suffering men embraced like long lost brothers. The heartless, embittered, tragically lonely hater of Christianity stared straight into the wondrous eyes of love...and melted. And he, too, became a lover of Christ.

It was that very night they both died. In the "death cell" it was death that usually got the last laugh. But, where there is love, it is Jesus that will surely triumph.[2]

Learning to Love

To love like that is supernatural! We can't love like that in our own will power, nor from our own resolve. Love like that is learned from the Great Lover Himself. And it is precisely that kind of love that must be the center of your love life. The essence of the "sweeter song" is this extraordinary love. Previously we spoke of the importance of trusting God. Trusting God is the key to unlocking the treasure chest. But once you open up the chest, you will discover the kind of *love* that is the sparkling secret to heavenly romance.

To learn *that kind* of love, you must first lean on the Great Lover. In leaning on Him and learning from Him, you will become a radiant example *of* Him for the entire world to see.

God has given me a wife who shows me Jesus' love. I like to tell people that each and every morning of my life I get the privilege of waking up to the likeness of Jesus Christ. In other words, in receiving her love I have come to understand in a greater way the love of my Lord.

I hope this doesn't come as too much of a shock but, I am not always a perfect saint. I know! Some of you just can't bring yourself to believe it. But it's true. In fact, if anyone would know, it's Leslie. She gets a different angle on my life than most. She calls my cranky and selfish bent my "poopy side." Now I am not proud that I have this "poopy side," but the reality is, God is not completely finished with me. I really do long to show the nature and character of Jesus to my wife and to the world at *all* times but...I still have my "poopy" moments.

There have been days when I am extremely unlovable. (I hope none of you can identify!) On days like that I think I end up saying, "I'm sorry Les!" an average of two hundred and seventy-three times (I keep good records). But I have a wife who has chosen *not* to keep records. Or maybe I should say, has chosen to throw out her score card instead of keeping it. No matter how cranky I have gotten, there has never been one time in our relationship that she has not forgiven me when I've asked. *I love being loved like that!* It's humbling, but it's life giving!

A Step Further

Slip into a room where you can be alone. Preferably to a place where there is total silence. Ask God to reveal to your heart and mind the great love He has for you. Then open your Bible to Luke chapters 23 and 24. Imagine that you have never before read this amazing story. Put yourself in a Jewish garment and give yourself a Hebrew accent. Walk with Jesus in this brief narrative. Feel the dust between your toes and hear the mêlée of the heartless throng about. Feel His pain, attempt to understand His agony, and really try to accept His extravagant love *that is just for you*. Finally, look into His sweet eyes in His hour of greatest suffering, and allow Him to ask you the question, "My child, are you willing to follow Me and love *like this?*"

Chapter Six

Leslie:
A Forever Kind of Love

Romance that's more than a feeling

The Gushy Stuff

Have you ever seen two people so hopelessly consumed with each other that they sit for hours, gazing into each other's eyes, unaware of time and space, and completely tuning out the world around them? It's the kind of thing that makes everyone else in the vicinity want to *gag*. It's the *gushy stuff!*

As Jan, a friend of mine, said of her dates with the man who would become her husband, "We wouldn't even watch the movie, we'd just sit and make 'googly eyes' at each other the whole time." *That* is definitely the *gushy stuff!*

Have you ever been so deliriously in love with someone that you turned into a total idiot? When Eric and I were engaged, we were idiotically in love. We were separated by 1,200 miles for most of that six-month period, and I am soooo glad no one recorded our phone conversations during that time! (They were *full* of the gushy stuff!)

One time while Eric was on a trip, he was staying at a house with a buddy named Ryan (a single guy who had no appreciation for what it means to be struck by the gushy stuff.) As soon as Eric thought the coast was clear, he sneaked away to call me late at night. As he was pouring out his heart to me in his classic "lovey-dovey" voice (that sounded like a mix between Kermit the Frog and Piglet from *Winnie the Pooh),* Ryan was behind the wall eavesdropping and dying with laughter at how stupid Eric sounded. Still to this day, Ryan hasn't let him (or me) forget that conversation! But Eric has a ready reply to Ryan's teasing, "Just wait till *you* fall in love, buddy! It'll be pay-back time!"

When we think of being "in love" with someone, usually the gushy stuff is what comes to our mind—the passionate, overwhelming feelings of adoration and devotion.

Another flame that usually fuels our passion for another person is the element of physical attraction. When we are young and carefree, we often base our feelings for another person on what our hormones tell us. When we are physically attracted to someone, every time they walk into a room where we are, our fire is lit and sparks fly inside of us.

Let's face it—the gushy stuff is fun. And where would any relationship be without an element of that idiotic kind of passion? But here is a question we all must face—*is the gushy stuff strong enough to build a lasting love upon?*

Happily Ever After?

In case you haven't noticed yet, the gushy stuff can be fairly unstable. One minute you can be so madly in love with someone you can't imagine life without them, and the next day you can wonder what you ever saw in them at all. Most of my dating relationships were nothing more than a roller coaster ride of emotions—the high points were when the gushy stuff was at its peak, the low points were when those feelings started to fade.

Another unstable factor is the element of physical beauty. Like the gushy stuff, physical attractiveness can be rather unstable. Beauty inevitably fades with time. I mean, when was the last time you saw a group of young men out on a Friday night turn their heads when a ninety-seven year old woman hobbled by on a walker? I *don't* think you'd hear whistles or exclamations of "Whoa! She's *hot!*" from these young potent males! Beauty does *not* last forever.

This used to worry me when I contemplated marriage. *If the gushy stuff comes and goes, and physical beauty fades with time, how do I know our love will last?*

And those concerns in this day and age are quite valid. Who would ever want to find someone they are head over heels in love with, ride off into the sunset together, live happily ever after...and then get divorced? Yet for too many couples, that fairy-tale-turned-nightmare hits all too close to home. Divorce is an epidemic that is sweeping our culture in unprecedented proportions.

In fact, studies show that the divorce rate among Christians has now *surpassed* non-Christians! *Get this!* Pollster George Barna recently released a study that shows those describing themselves as "born-again" Christians actually have a *higher* divorce rate than do those that claim no belief in Jesus Christ.[1]

As we look ahead toward marriage someday, is there any way to prevent us from becoming one more statistic? How can we know that our God-written love story will last for a lifetime?

The answer lies in the *kind* of love upon which we choose to build a relationship. If we build it on the gushy stuff or base it on physical attraction, we most certainly are headed for divorce, because one day we may wake up and realize those feelings aren't there anymore.

Someone once told me, "Dating is great preparation for marriage. By dating around, you learn what you want in a marriage partner."

As much as I liked that statement, I soon realized that dating around *wasn't* preparing me very well for marriage. In fact, if I were to be honest, it was setting me up better for *divorce!* On a whim, I would dive headfirst into a relationship, pour on a heavy dose of the gushy stuff, and then when those feelings faded, I'd go out and find someone new—a constant cycle of *temporary* relationships. But God didn't intend for marriage to be temporary. And by living this way, I wasn't preparing to love one man for a lifetime...I was preparing to have multiple short-lived, emotion-based romantic flings.

True Love

There is another love, a higher love that *is* strong enough to build a lifelong relationship upon. It is the same love that the Romanian Christian demonstrated toward his persecutor in prison. It is, in fact, the very same love God had for us when He sacrificed His only Son to die in our place. And it is not based on feelings or physical desires. It is based on *a choice.* A commitment that says, "I will seek your highest good above my own. I will lay down my life for you."

When Eric and I promised each other that we would stay together for life—no matter if he loses his hair or gets a belly, or if I burn all his meals—we knew we could keep this commitment, because it was based not on feelings but on *a choice.*

Don't get me wrong, the gushy stuff and physical attraction are a fun and exciting part of any healthy relationship. But in our culture, passionate emotions and physical desires are the *entire basis* for almost every romantic relationship. No wonder marriages are crumbling left and right!

We need to think of the gushy stuff as merely the icing on the cake...it's what adds that extra dimension of flavor to a relationship. But it's *not* the ingredient that keeps a romance together. If we don't have a lasting love and commitment for our spouse as the foundation of our relationship, we don't have anything at all.

If anyone should know how to love with lasting love, it should be Christians. We have the very example of Jesus Christ Himself from which to pattern our lives and our love toward others. We have the Great Lover Himself enabling us to love like He does! Why do we so often neglect spilling that kind of love over into this crucial area...our love life?

Love That Lasts Through the Storms

Karen and Scott had been happily married for about ten years when something happened that changed their lives forever. Scott, a respected businessman, was driving to work when he collided with a large truck pulling a two-ton trailer. In the accident the trailer landed on top of his car, pinning him underneath. He suffered a severe blow to the head.

At the hospital, Karen learned that Scott had extensive brain damage. He would no longer be able to think or communicate as an adult. In fact, he didn't even remember who she was at first.

Over the following weeks and months, Karen had to adjust to seeing her husband confined to a wheelchair and speaking and acting like a child. He had to be fed, washed, dressed...he was no longer the capable man she had married.

Most of us wouldn't have blamed Karen at all if she had simply put Scott into a nursing home and gotten on with her life. After all, he could no longer meet any of her needs, and it was a huge burden upon her to care for him when he was like this.

But, as Karen puts it, "I remembered that on our wedding day I had made a commitment to Scott...and a commitment isn't meant to be broken!"

So for years, she has faithfully served Scott, loving him even when he didn't remember her, helping him when he couldn't help her back. Today, Scott has made tremendous progress in his condition, yet he still remains physically impaired. He is always in need of Karen's faithful love, help, and support, and she is faithful to give it. How incredibly beautiful! This is heroic Christ-like love in action. This is the kind of love Christian marriages *should* be made of!

A Simple Glass of Water

Unconditional love can be demonstrated in far less dramatic ways as well. Since Eric and I have been married, I have offered him plenty of opportunities to test his unconditional love for me! He has seen me sick in bed with a mountain of Kleenex on the floor. He has seen me in my very worst of moods, as I childishly storm around the house and slam doors, just to let everyone know I'm having a bad day. He has seen me without my hair brushed or my make-up on when I first wake up in the morning (not a pretty sight!) and he still loves me!

I don't know what it is, but it seems that every time we are tucked in bed with the lights off, and just before we drift off to sleep…I get thirsty. At this point I am way too comfortable and drowsy to get up and get a glass of water for myself! So, in my very best, pitiful puppy-dog voice I beseech my beloved husband,

"Beef? I need some water."

He doesn't have to respond. He could easily pretend to be asleep or simply say, "Get it yourself, kiddo." But that's not what he does. After a groggy "Huh? Um…okay," he heroically arises from the warm bed and staggers to the kitchen to fetch me a glass of water. No complaints. No grumbling. Just pure, unconditional love in action.

I wouldn't recommend putting unconditional love to the test just for the fun of it. (The water thing is pushing it, I'll admit.) But it is wonderful to know that my relationship with Eric is based on that kind of love…for a lifetime.

All the Days of My Life

Not long after my decision to "give God the pen" to write my love story, I learned a truth about loving my future husband that dramatically changed the way I was living.

I was innocently reading my "proverb for the day" which happened to be Proverbs 31. The famous chapter in the Bible that describes the "wife of godly character."

I must admit I wasn't paying very close attention or taking the words too seriously. After all, I figured most of it wouldn't apply to me until *after* I was a "wife," which as far as I was concerned, wouldn't be for awhile! Yet suddenly my eye fell upon a verse, and the words stood out to me.

She (the wife of godly character) *does him* (her husband) *good and not evil all the days of her life.* (Prov. 31:12 NIV)

Wait a minute! My mind raced. *All the days of her life?* What was that supposed to mean? I had yet to meet any woman who had been married *all* the days of her life. Did this verse mean she tried to do her husband good…even *before* she met him?

I felt a gentle nudge on my heart. And somehow, I knew this was what God wanted for me. To seek my future husband's highest good…*starting right now.*

"How can I love someone I've never met?" I argued back inside my head. "I mean, I'm keeping a commitment to abstinence for my future husband…so what else can I possibly do for him?"

The gentle nudge continued, ultimately forcing me to examine the way I was living. How had I been approaching relationships? Each time I was involved with someone, I poured my heart, my emotions, my affection, my time, and all my attention onto that person. Not to mention the fact, that though I may have been technically a virgin, I wasn't keeping myself physically pure—I was constantly compromising my standards.

"How would your future husband feel..." my heart seemed to ask, "if he could see you giving everything you are to these relationships? If he could watch you freely giving away your heart, your emotions, and your physical purity...a treasure that belongs to him?"

My heart ached. I realized so clearly in that moment that I hadn't been loving my future husband. With the way I had been living, I hadn't even been considering him at all! Instead, I had been consumed with meeting my own immediate desires. Sadness overcame me as I saw that I had been giving his treasure, piece by piece, to each guy I dated.

"Lord, I want to honor You and my future husband with the way I live," I prayed that day, "and I am making a commitment today to love him and seek his highest good from now on."

My love life was transformed. Even though I didn't know him yet, I began truly loving Eric at that moment—truly loving my future husband "all the days of my life." It wasn't always easy. At times it was painful. And of course, there were plenty of moments when the old selfishness tried to creep back in. But with God's help, I started laying the foundation for a lifelong relationship, because I was willing to start loving my future husband with a sacrificial love, a selfless love, a lasting love...an unconditional love.

A Step Further

Sneak away to a private place. Put on some romantic background music, and prayerfully read First Corinthians 13. Ponder all the qualities of true Christlike love, all the markings of a heavenly lover. Are you consumed with self-love or *selfless* love? Are you willing to learn to love sacrificially? Pray and ask God to teach you how to love with extravagance, even when it's difficult and painful.

Chapter Seven

Eric:
Developing Inward Excellence

Purity that goes beyond skin-deep

An Invaluable Ninety-One Cent Lesson

Hey, Eric!" Steve yelled as I was getting comfortable in the yellow plastic McDonald's booth. "Bob's picking the Huskers to beat your Buffs by twenty!"

"What?" I screeched. "Bob, your Huskers will be lucky to come out of Folsom Field *alive*, let alone with a victory!"

Ah...those memorable college days. I get teary-eyed just reminiscing about them. There I was with my buddies, who like me were once again dateless on yet another Friday night. To ease our egos, we all headed to our favorite hangout to splurge our carefully budgeted spare ninety-one cents on a sumptuous chocolate-vanilla swirl cone and engage in some serious "guy talk."

For all of you female readers out there who are interested in discovering how guys tick, just listen up. Whenever we guys huddle together in a plastic yellow booth, we become very predictable, at least as conversation is concerned.

First we talk about sports. We argue, grunt, sweat, flex, and all sorts of tough things like that. Once we exhaust that topic, we start talking about another one of our favorite subjects...food!

"Did you know that Zips is selling five cheeseburgers for two bucks now?"

At that we ooh and aah.

"Well, *I* just bought twenty Top Ramens for two bucks at Rosauers!"

With that announcement we all yell out, "No way, Dude!"

Eventually we cover all the important bases regarding our digestive system, and we move on to our endocrine system (the place where all our hormones hang out).

I think it happened at precisely the same moment that Bob excitedly roared out the news about the "gorgeous blonde" from Sweeney Hall who was proofreading his paper on "Ducks and Deadly Diseases." I felt a little knock upon my heart.

"Clank, Clank!"

It was *God*, reminding me of His position in this all-so-important area of my life. It had been a few months since I "let go of my pen," and still, at times, I was struggling with trusting Him.

"Clank, Clank!"

I had experienced some moments of serious doubt as to the reliability of God in the area of romance. But as He again knocked this fateful Friday night, I was reminded of not only the fact that I had entrusted Him with the pen of my love life, but that He had given me a little something, too. He had given me *a beautiful hope*. It was a hope that He was preparing a special someone to perfectly match my life!

"Clank, Clank!"

I remember drifting off into LaLa Land as Bob shared how his "gorgeous blonde" gently touched his hand after she found a grammatical error in the opening line of his "Ducks and Deadly Diseases" essay. I was physically present with my college buddies at that plastic table, but my mind was on another planet. For the first time in my life I was beginning to realize, that if God's plan and purpose for my life really was marriage, then the person I was going to one day marry was most likely *somewhere* on this great big planet. And right at that moment she was doing *something!* I was swallowed up in one gigantic thought...*she's alive!*

Have you ever thought about that? Just ponder it for a moment. If God's plan and purpose for you is marriage, then *that person you will one day marry* (unless they are not born yet) is alive and wandering the earth. If that's true, if they are really out there somewhere, don't you wonder what they are doing?

That's precisely what I thought.

"I wonder what she is doing tonight?"

I pondered the fact that it was a Friday night and that there was a full moon in the sky. I wondered if she was looking at the same moon I was and maybe even thinking of me. Everything was lovely. Then it hit me.

"She'd better not be with a *guy!*"

My mind was filled with a grotesque picture of some geekish Val Kilmer-look-alike slinking his snake-like arm around my future wife's shoulder, and whispering with his disgusting voice, "Doesn't the moon look peachy, Babe?"

Then, as if it could get any worse, I imagined this sweet talking Turkey puckering his unbridled and oversized lips and...*kissing* my future wife!

My lips twisted into a crazed snarl and my eyes boiled with fury. My right hand formed a pulsating fist and smacked my open left hand with savage force.

I was ready to *kill* this guy! He was touching something that was solely *mine!*

I'm glad there wasn't a video camera on me as I sat there in that plastic booth. My buddies and I never talked about it afterward (believe me, I didn't dare bring it up). Maybe they thought my little tirade was an allergic reaction to ice cream cone dust or something. But on a night where I blew a whopping ninety-one cents on something that I enjoyed for only five-and-a-half minutes, I also gained an invaluable little truth that I will enjoy for the rest of my life.

As this disturbing picture of my future wife and "the imposter" filled my head, God "Clank, Clanked" upon my heart. It was almost as if His great big fatherly arm wrapped itself around my shoulder. In a way only God can, He nudged my heart and slipped me a little note.

"Eric," this imaginary note read, "you desire purity in your wife, don't you?"

"You better believe it, I do!" I trumpeted in response. "I want my wife to be *pure!*"

"That's great, Eric!" The note continued, "I'm glad you are interested in purity. I'm quite a fan of it Myself!"

It was then that I learned the life-lesson.

"Just think, Eric! If you desire purity in your wife, how much more do you think she desires purity...*in you*?

The Donny Lucero Effect

I guess it happened somewhere in junior high, between a Donny Lucero lecture on the "looseness" of girls and an informal discussion that I overheard among the cheerleaders about how someone needed to invent a female condom so that girls could have more control in a sexual relationship. I guess I finally just came to the decision that there wasn't a girl in the whole wide world who was going to set herself aside for me.

We can call it the "Donny Lucero effect." Our desire for something beautiful is strong at first. We long, we believe, and we even wait for this "something beautiful," sort of like we do with the Tooth Fairy and Santa. But we all have our moments when we finally grasp "reality." We never see it, we never hear of it, and we never sniff even the slightest scent that this "something beautiful" even exists. Then finally, there comes a moment in our life when Donny Lucero's words are that last piece of straw that finally breaks the backbone of our once confident desire.

"I've had it!" we mutter under our breaths with a disgusted grimace. "I'm not going to save something for someone whose not saving something for me!"

The Donny Lucero effect got me, and I wouldn't doubt but it has gotten a good many of you, too. I mean, why would I go to all the trouble of denying my desires for so many years, if the person I'm doing it for isn't doing the same for me. What a waste!

An Oily Dirtball Like Donny

I pondered my love life as I sat in that plastic booth that memorable Friday night. I pondered what it meant to truly love someone, and what it meant to be pure.

For years I had wanted the world around me to think I was "the sex machine." Here I was a virgin, but I wanted people to think I wasn't. If you had set both Jesus Christ and wormy little Donny Lucero in front of me and said,

"Eric, we'll give you a choice. You can be shaped into the likeness and share the same nature with either the King of the Universe or with this oily dirtball over here named Donny. Which would you prefer? Consider wisely, Eric, because you'll have to live with your decision."

It is very humbling for me to admit this, but up until this point in my life, I would have probably chosen the oily dirtball over my precious Jesus. Donny's life seemed so appealing on the outside. It seemed his every desire was met, his every craving thoroughly enjoyed. What I didn't take into account was his empty and purposeless life, endlessly searching for meaning, acceptance, and...love.

Purity Is a Sweeter Song

With God tenderly standing by my side, I finished the little note He had slipped me. The last line read,

"It is more *blessed* to give [Eric] than to receive" (Acts 20:35 NIV).

It was the "sweeter song" all over again! That word "blessed"—that same word that illuminates the way to *supreme happiness!* It was found in thinking about what I could *give* instead of what I could *get.*

My whole life I had wanted my future spouse to do me the favor of staying pure, give me a little respect, and prove to me that I'm the love of her life. I was hungering for the "beautiful side of love," but I never realized that I would find it when I started to focus on the way *I* lived and loved and not on the way *she* lived and loved. And that I would find it, when I finally focused on honoring her *before we met* even if she *never considered* honoring me in return.

My invaluable ninety-one cent lesson was this:

"Eric? Do you really want that "sweeter song"? Then set your life aside as a priceless treasure, kept polished and pure, for your future spouse. When she one day receives that gift, there won't be a love song in all the earth that will be able to express the tender love and romance of such a moment...only heaven could play a melody sweet enough!"

That very scenario was played out two thousand years ago by a Bridegroom, named Jesus, for His Bride. The universe has never been the same!

Rotten Mangos

Your entire body, everything from your heart, to your mind, to the skin that holds it all in place, is a treasure. For some reason, our generation of Christians only views purity as an external thing—as long as we're not having sex, we are supposedly "pure."

"I'm just reading the articles!"

Oh, yes! The famous quote never to be forgotten throughout the history of McDuffey Hall. Spoken like a true "guy" when he was brought before the self-appointed college morality board with a *Playboy* magazine in hand. The rest of the quote went something like,

"How ridiculous! I'm not looking at the *pictures!*"

Well, every guy who has ever salivated over baby back ribs on an empty stomach can join me in saying, "Yeah, right!"

Purity goes beyond skin deep. There isn't an honest man alive who would deny it. People are like mangos. It is very common for a terribly rotten mango to look perfectly healthy on the outside, but I wouldn't recommend eating it. And I wouldn't recommend marrying a rotten mango either. They might look scrumptious on the outside, but more than just your stomach will be upset if you say, "I do."

Some Guy Talk

Give this warped world a little taste of heaven on earth by graciously accepting the hand life deals you. In the dense, immoral fog of this generation, shine your life as a beacon, guiding others to the goodness and grace of God. Though this world is polluted, live in spotless purity, uncontaminated by all the garbage around you.

Philippians 2:14-15 (paraphrase)

Guys, just imagine that God has it in His mind to bring into your life someday a precious and lovely wife who will make your heart skip a beat every time you look at her. Can you picture that?

Now, I want you also to imagine that this beautiful young woman can see you right now. Pretend that she is capable of watching you, *everywhere* you go, and she is able to see *everything* you do. I know this is really stretching your imagination, guys, but stick with me!

Okay then, if she could see and hear *everything*, ask yourself this question, "If she followed me around throughout my day, every day of my life, would she feel cherished and adored by me as she watches me interact with other girls? Would she come away each day saying, 'He sure does love me!' or would she be deeply hurt by the way I give what is hers to other women?"

For instance, what if I was spending a Friday night with a perfumed little lady instead of with my dateless buddies. What if my future spouse could see me slithering my snake-like arm around another girl's shoulder? What if she could witness me puckering my unbridled and oversized lips and kissing someone else? Do you think she would be cheering me on?

"Go Eric! Man alive, he is going to be one *incredible* kisser! I can't wait for my turn!"

I don't think so! In fact, I know exactly how Leslie would respond to such a scene. She would have wet eyes and a crushed heart because I was giving my love and affection to someone other than her.

Marriage vows are a heavy-duty thing! In front of a whole crowd of witnesses you are announcing your love and your life-long faithfulness to your wife. Whether in sickness or in health, make-up on or make-up off, *you're committed*. Many of us guys wait until that very last possible moment to be committed to that special woman. That's sort of like not ever touching a basketball in your life and then trying out for the Harlem Globetrotters. You'll shoot a lot of air balls in life that way. The secret to heavenly romance is to begin practicing purity for a woman and cherishing her with your thoughts, actions, and words, *long* before you even meet her.

It was my goal, from the night I blew my whopping ninety-one cents, to begin to live as if she could see me. I wanted to adore her and cherish her before I even met her.

And I realized I could do that by choosing, in every situation life brought my way, to think of her as if she were right beside me and to consider how my decisions would affect her.

Six months before our wedding, Leslie made a statement to me that made me shudder. She simply said,

"Eric, I wish you had never had a desire for another girl in your *entire* life!"

Now how would you, as a guy, respond to a statement like that? Whether or not that is an unrealistic request for a woman to have is beside the point. The point is this, the *desire* she had (and your future wife has right now, even though you don't yet know her) is that you would be a "one-woman man" your *entire* life, not just *after* you meet her.

Give her your heart, mind, and body *now!* It's easy to run around from one shallow relationship to the next meeting your own selfish desires. But it takes a real man, a real lover, to keep one woman satisfied *for life*. I guarantee you, the rewards of such a decision are off the charts amazing. And she'll love you like a man longs to be loved.

But, What If?

There's just one enormous question still hanging in the air.

"What if I *don't* get married? What if it isn't in God's mind and heart for me to ever take wedding vows in the first place? Why would what I do now matter, if my future spouse isn't even there to watch?"

That's a fair question. I mean, it's one thing to set aside all of those desires if they one day will be satisfied in marriage, but what if they *never* are?

One of the richest and most priceless things we can learn is this simple truth: Even if we *never* get married, *nothing* we do in guarding our hearts, filtering our thoughts, and cherishing our future spouse by the way we live will be wasted. It is *not* merely for our future marriage here on earth that we do these things, it is also an investment in our glorious future marriage in heaven with Jesus.

Mattering far beyond what our future spouse thinks or feels, is what our tender Savior and gentle Lord Jesus thinks and feels. Does He have wet eyes as He watches our lives?

For most of my life I followed in the footsteps of Donny Lucero instead of Christ. I thank Jesus that He was patient with me and didn't base His commitment to me on *my loyalty* to Him. He had many days in which His eyes were wet with tears shed over my reckless ways. But I'm with Him now, listening to a "sweeter song," learning to love Leslie the way He first loved me. And I wouldn't trade ten million difficult footsteps of following Christ for even one sleazy little shuffle of Donny Lucero's feet.

> *Even more love. That is what I pray God will give you. That your love life would make Jesus proud, abundantly filled with an intimate knowledge of the Truth, as well as the necessary tools to discern the very finest and best. And that you would make Jesus stunningly beautiful and superbly believable to everyone you encounter, gathering praise and applause for the God of the Universe.*
>
> Philippians 1: 9-11 (paraphrase)

A Step Further

Aren't there times in your life when you wish you could crawl into the mind of God? Well, open up your Bible to Matthew chapter 5 and get a little taste of what it is like to know the way the God of the Universe thinks. As you read the words of Jesus Himself, you will find that God's ways are totally different from ours. Where we humans value external gain and external good looks, God looks past it all and applauds *internal* gain and *internal* good looks. Ask yourself if you have been putting the emphasis in the right place in your life.

Chapter Eight

Leslie:
Heart Matters

A female angle on inward excellence

W hen my mom was thirteen, she was still playing with a Chatty Cathy Doll and had yet to try on her first pair of high heels. Times have changed. By the time I was thirteen I was hanging out at the mall while being offered cigarettes and beer. That's not all I was offered. At thirteen, I also received my first opportunity to have sex.

I had known Bryan, a gangly fifteen-year old in baggy Umbros who thought he was *Knight Rider* in teenage form, for approximately two days when he called me up out of the blue with a "romantic proposition." It went something like this:

"Hi, Lisa," he mumbled while making a grotesque smacking noise as he chomped a potato chip.

"My name's *Leslie,*" I corrected.

"Oh yeah, sorry, I forgot." He floundered as he stifled a burp. "Anyway, I really like you and I was just wondering, when do you think we can have sex?"

Oh, Bryan, you know just what to say to take a girl's breath away!

Fortunately, I had been raised on a healthy dose of the "abstinence" philosophy, and growing up in the church I had learned that "true love waits." I successfully practiced the "just say no" tactic on Bryan-the-sleaze-ball, and he conveniently disappeared from my life. But from that time on, opportunities to give away my virginity were never ending.

When my mom was in high school, the popular crowd looked down on "easy" girls. It was completely normal and accepted to graduate from high school as a virgin. By the time *I* got to high school, the school nurses were handing out contraceptives in the halls, and the only reason someone would graduate a virgin was if he or she was a social misfit.

In the world I lived in, sexual temptation wasn't something that just lurked around dark corners...sexual temptation was constantly in your face. Nearly all of my friends were sexually active—and told me of their exploits on a regular basis. I knew couples at school who would go to their cars during lunch or breaks and have sex during the school day. And of course, every party I went to was all about sneaking off with your latest fling to experiment sexually. In the halls at school, girls would be touched and grabbed by guys in ways that would have made our parents blush a generation ago. Yet we were trained to laugh it off, even encourage it. Any girl trying to "keep her purity" was laughed at and labeled a prude...and was presumably thought of as undesirable to most guys.

The Abstinence Approach

In the midst of all this, there came a wave of Christian teaching about purity in the form of abstinence seminars, books with guidelines for "Christian dating," and promise rings. It came in many different packages, but the basic message went something like this:

"Kids, don't have sex before marriage. You need to respect yourself and your future spouse. Sex will be so much more beautiful if you wait till marriage. Protect yourself from STDs, pregnancy, and heartache. Abstinence is cool! Thousands of young people are committed to waiting...why don't you wait, too?"

Somewhere along the way, between my mom and dad's parental exhortation, and my youth pastor's "purity pep rallies," I got the message that my virginity was a treasure to save for my future husband. I tried to accept the concept that someday there would be a man who would appreciate the fact that I had remained a virgin for him. Even though I didn't see one eligible guy in my life who seemed to want a "pure" young woman, I was assured that men like that *did* exist.

My commitment to purity became the heroic declaration, "I'm not gonna have sex till marriage." I hoped my husband would appreciate such a sacrifice someday! In the meantime, I was going to go out there and date for fun, live it up, have a great time, go to the edge, enjoy relationships, and then later down the road I'd meet Mr. Right and forget about every other boyfriend I'd ever had. I was sure that as long as I didn't have sex, surely my future husband, parents, church leaders, and even God would have to be impressed.

Temporary Flings Equal Permanent Damage

I found out quickly that my dating life was *not* going to be the blissful experience I had imagined it would be. No one had prepared me for the emotional pain involved in this lifestyle. The first time a boyfriend broke up with me, I thought I was having a complete emotional breakdown! I cried for months. It felt like someone had reached inside my heart and ripped it out, then shattered it on the ground into a million pieces. I had never known such pain.

To fill the aching, empty void inside me after that traumatic experience, I began a desperate search for another boyfriend. And thus began the vicious cycle. Each time a relationship ended, whether it had been serious or casual, long-term or only two weeks long, I felt crushed emotionally.

Dating became like an addictive drug to me—I used relationships to help me feel confident and secure in life. If I was ever *without* a relationship, I became agitated, restless, and insecure. So I made sure those times were rare.

The longer I was in a relationship, the more of myself— my energy, my time, my affection, and my emotion—I poured into the guy I was dating. We would stay on the phone for hours each night, discussing dreams, fears, and desires, and, of course, declaring our love and passion for each other. We would spend every minute of free time together. We could be found in the hallway between classes entangled in each other's arms. In some cases, I felt like I was all but married to the guy I was dating.

Damaged Treasure

All this time I thought of myself as "pure" because I was holding on (for dear life at times!) to my virginity. Whenever I dated someone, I tried to make sure that the guy I went out with shared the same conviction I did.

"Oh, sure, Babe, I believe in abstinence until marriage, too," they would always assure me with an irresistible smile before we launched into a passionate make-out session.

But I didn't feel pure. Deep down, nothing about these temporary, shallow dating relationships felt right. I had always longed for a "Knight in Shining Armor" to sweep me off my feet, to cherish me like a princess, to honor me. As a starry-eyed young girl I had expected dating to be a beautiful, romantic experience in which I would feel treasured and loved.

This animalistic, physical passion from guys who did not truly know me or care about me was *not* the fulfillment of my romantic dreams. I didn't feel cherished. I felt used. I felt dirty. Especially those times when I had given so much of myself to a relationship, and then after it ended, I had to see that guy with another girl, ignoring me as if I didn't exist.

In spite of the emphasis in the Christian circles on purity being equal to "virginity," I began to realize there *had* to be more to it than just not having sex. Otherwise, I wouldn't feel so defiled every time I gave my heart and physical body to a guy. I had thought of "losing my purity" as a forbidden line I was never to cross. But after painful reflection, the truth burned deep into my heart—*in getting as close to that line as I possibly could, I had lost something already.*

Emotional? Who, Me?

As women, one of the greatest gifts we possess is our heart—our emotions, our sensitive nature, and our femininity. It comes naturally for us to pour ourselves into a relationship, to become emotionally wrapped up in the guy we are dating, to revolve our world around him. That's not always true with a guy. A man may not be as tempted to open his heart to someone—in fact, he may not even know how. He doesn't usually build his life around the girl he's dating. It's very common for a guy to get involved physically without getting involved emotionally at all.

A familiar scenario during high school was the girl who came to me in tears, devastated because she had given herself away emotionally and physically to a guy, only to find out later that he was just using her for sex. She thought he loved her. He thought she was easy prey.

And then came another scenario as I grew older, this one a little more surprising. Instead of girls letting themselves be used like sex objects by guys, *the girls* became the ones who went out looking for a conquest.

"He's got a bo-dy! I think I'll have sex with him this weekend," was a casual comment I often heard from girlfriends, usually communicated to me in terms just a little more graphic.

They shut off their emotions. They subconsciously told themselves that the only way to be protected from heartbreak was to deny they had a heart and revert to the same animalistic, noncommittal physical passion they had seen in the guys they dated.

But that approach can only work for so long before the pain breaks through the wall of protection around the heart. As women, we are *designed* to give ourselves completely—emotionally and physically to *one* man. And there is a deep need inside of us to be loved and cherished for a lifetime by the man to whom we give that gift.

Physical purity can't be separated from our emotions. It's a package deal. When we give ourselves to someone emotionally, it leads right to the next step...giving ourselves to him physically.

I will never forget hearing an unmarried friend of mine describe why she gave her virginity away to a guy she'd been "in love" with for years.

"I gave my heart to Matt," she told me. "I poured my life into him. I couldn't imagine giving my virginity to anyone else—he already had the rest of me, so I decided to give him the whole package."

Even if we try to set our emotions aside and merely "conquer" a guy physically, whether we like it or not, our emotions *do* get involved. Trying to ignore that delicate, vulnerable and emotional part of us is to deny the very fabric of our being as women.

Maybe you have learned the hard lesson that casually giving yourself away physically causes incredible pain—you feel guilty, dirty, and used afterwards.

But have you ever thought of your *heart* as a treasure every bit as valuable as your physical purity? Have you ever felt the pain that comes from casually giving away your heart? From pouring all of yourself into someone—only to have that precious treasure thrown on to the ground and trampled?

Hamburger Heart

When I had that Proverbs 31 experience I mentioned previously, and made the commitment to honor my future husband with the way I lived, I had to face a shocking realization. I really had *not* been keeping myself pure at all. I had been taking the treasure of my heart and emotions and spending it carelessly on temporary relationships.

How much of your treasure will be left, came a soft whisper to my heart, *if you continue to give it away, piece by piece in one relationship after another?*

I knew that eventually I would meet my future husband, and that I would want to love him with all that was in me. But how could I offer my whole heart to my husband someday if it was nothing but a used, battered, and broken mess?

As Carrie, a distraught sophomore in college described it, "I've been in so many relationships and been hurt so many times that my heart is nothing but hamburger-meat now."

I can relate to that statement. In fact, I don't know many girls who haven't been through a "hamburger heart" experience.

Priceless Pearl

As women, we are given a great gift. Our purity. And everything that makes us who we are emotionally—our feminine nature, our sensitivity, our vulnerability, and our desire to give ourselves fully to one man—is part of that gift. Our purity is a treasure. It is so much more than just our physical virginity...it starts with who we are on the *inside*. It is like a priceless pearl, tucked safely away in a protective shell, growing and becoming more beautiful with time.

In my dating relationships, I damaged my precious pearl of purity. I felt dirty and used because of it. But the damage didn't just happen when I "went a little too far" physically. Giving away this treasure started the moment I gave away my heart and emotions to men who were never meant to receive that gift. I had been careless with my treasure. I had *allowed* my heart to become battered and broken.

I used to think that the unbearable devastation of "breaking up" with a boyfriend was just a natural part of the dating process. But there was nothing natural about it! It was a pain God never meant for me to experience. The valuable and delicate pearl of my purity had been ripped too soon from its protective shell, then tossed back, damaged and bruised.

A One-Man Woman

One of the greatest ways we can love our future husbands with unconditional, self-sacrificing love is by carefully protecting that precious gift we possess—our inward and outward purity. Purity is more than just avoiding the "forbidden line" of giving away our virginity. As women, we can pour ourselves into developing inward excellence—becoming a beautiful, whole, undefiled treasure from the inside out. We will have so much more to offer our future husbands if we do. It doesn't mean we will always be perfect, but it does mean that we will be headed in the right direction...on a path not of compromise, but of radiant and joyful purity in its truest form.

Ann, one of my closest friends, is a beautiful, graceful brunette and a sophomore at a Christian college in Illinois. Her concept of purity is completely different than mine was growing up. At nineteen, she has never been in a dating relationship, never given her heart away; never even been kissed! Extreme? Impossible? Miserable? Not quite.

Ann decided from a young age that she wanted to offer a treasure of purity to her husband on her wedding day. But this was not just another "abstinence commitment." This was a choice to carefully guard her heart, her emotions, her physical purity, and everything she was, for the man she would one day marry. Ann's goal is to offer herself fully and completely, with no excess baggage, to her husband someday.

During her youth she allowed her Maker to care for and develop that precious pearl of her purity, so it will become a sparkling, glistening, and untarnished gem for her husband. And she asked her Lord to guard and protect her delicate heart in His hands.

She is not a social misfit. She is confidant in who she is, enthusiastic about life, and even pretty enough to be a model. Needless to say, the guy who ends up with a woman like her had better be pretty incredible!

Because Ann has been so careful with her treasure, she's not tempted to blow such a valuable gift on the first Mr. Charm who comes her way. The man she marries is going to have to *win* her heart first.

"As for guys pursuing me for temporary relationships," she says, "my attitude is, 'I'm already taken.' Until God brings my future husband along and I know it's him, I'm not available."

What a difference from the attitude *I* had when I was throwing my heart around like a Nerf ball! My precious pearl had been "up for grabs" to the highest bidder (or the best looking), and as a result, it did not reach its full potential for beauty. Ann, on the other hand, has tucked her treasure safely into the hands of God, not to be retrieved until He shows her it's time.

It's not that Ann has never made a mistake. It's not that she has never struggled with living out her commitment. She will be the first to admit that she is very human. She deals with the same frustrations, temptations, fears, and doubts that all of us do. There are moments of extreme loneliness. She has wondered at times if her standards are too high, if her commitment is really worth it. And she acknowledges that the only thing that has gotten her this far has been leaning heavily upon her Savior each and every day.

But Ann's decision represents the kind of standard we all should strive for, with God's help. *Becoming a one-man woman.* Loving our future husbands with the way we live and the way we guard our pearl of purity...*all the days of our lives.* Not out of obligation, but out of unconditional love for our future spouse and a deep desire to honor our Maker.

Two people who have saved themselves completely—inwardly, outwardly, emotionally, and physically—coming together to love each other for a lifetime with the purest, most uninhibited love imaginable...this is romance in its truest form! This is God's perfect design for you! This is the "sweeter song"! And it's something we can begin to work toward right now!

Many of us have damaged our pearl of purity. Many of us have even given away our treasure completely. Even if this is your story, it's not too late, by the grace of God, to start walking a different path. It's not too late to discover a God-written love story. It's time to allow God to mold you into His likeness. As we let God have His way, we will be transformed into a princess of true purity.

What a Real Man Wants

"But what if there isn't a guy out there who really *wants* a princess of purity?" Let's face it girls, this is the question that runs through the minds of thousands of Christian young women.

And I understand why. In our culture, purity in any way shape or form is not valued, and especially not by men. We are persuaded to think that men like "easy women," and they don't want to waste their time with those who play "hard to get."

It seems that anytime I have known a woman with a commitment to purity, one of her biggest struggles is that the men in her life are always trying to get her to lower her standards. Even most Christian men do not seem to fully appreciate a woman's desire to guard her heart and protect her purity. It's an unending battle for a woman to hold onto her treasure, and then she begins to even wonder if it's worth it. What if guys really *aren't* looking for that kind of purity in a woman?

I once overheard a conversation between four godly young men about what they were looking for in a woman.

"A woman who has mystery—who guards her heart and isn't easy to get."

"A woman with backbone. High standards."

"A woman who is focused on God and isn't easily distracted by men."

"A woman who doesn't throw herself at me, but allows me to win her heart over time."

I couldn't resist asking a few questions....

"So do you guys all want a woman who is committed to purity?"

A chorus of emphatic affirmative responses filled the air.

"And what's your opinion of girls who are easy?"

"It's disgusting."

"A turn-off."

"Totally unattractive."

"How do you feel about a girl who is careful about guarding her emotions?"

"I have the utmost respect for a girl like that."

"That's the kind of girl I'd want to marry."

"If I'm interested in a girl, it may be frustrating if she doesn't fall for me right away, but deep down I am all the more intrigued by the challenge of winning her heart."

These are *real* responses from *real* men. What I discovered that day is that the kind of men who are worth waiting for really *do* exist. And they really *are* looking for a princess of purity. I have since had similar discussions with hundreds of eligible Christ-focused young men of real integrity. And I have yet to meet one who is *not* longing for a woman of true purity. Men who go after easy women for another "score" are just looking to feed their flesh. They are not looking for true love, and they certainly aren't worthy of your time and attention.

A *real* man, the kind of man a woman wants to give her life to, is one who will respect her dignity, who will honor her like the valuable treasure she is. A *real* man will not attempt to rip her precious pearl from its protective shell, or persuade her with charm to give away her treasure prematurely, but he will wait patiently until she willingly gives him the prize of her heart. A *real* man will cherish and care for that precious prize forever.

It's too bad that women have to work overtime just to protect their hearts these days. If we had more *real* men who treat women as God intended, it wouldn't be so difficult! But even if real men are hard to find, they do exist, and they are worth waiting for. So don't get discouraged on your journey of inward excellence. To real men, your purity is *beautiful,* and it will be highly esteemed someday.

My brother-in-law, Mark, is single. At twenty-six, he is an attractive, talented, and godly man. He captured well what a *real* man is looking for in a woman when he declared,

"I don't want a woman who just turns my head...but a woman who turns my *heart.*"

Just think...if God has planned marriage for your life, there is one real man who might be dreaming of his princess of purity at this very moment.

A Step Further

God created women with an aura of mystery about them. The world is always trying to unwrap it and steal it, but a woman of God knows how to protect the treasure that God has entrusted to her. Prayerfully read Luke 1:26-28 and Luke 2:8-20, the story of a young woman who trusted God, waited on God, and cherished His promises to her. Girls, as you read this story, ask yourself what it's worth to God to guard the treasure entrusted to you. And guys, as you read this story, ask yourself how you might do better at helping the women in your life protect their mystery.

Section Three
Waiting for a Love Story

Chapter Nine

Eric:
The Art of Faithfulness

*A skill to learn long
before the wedding vows*

Romantic Goodness

I remember learning the basics of how to treat a girl when I was seven. Her name was Emily and she was "yuck!" Nasty little Emily was solely responsible for scribbling on my 1978 Denver Bronco's team picture. She was also the intolerable human being who spilled girly perfume on my pillow case (it's no wonder I kissed it later in life). And worst of all, she called me a "Doofhead" in front of my good buddy Stevie.

I'll never forget the lecture I received from my mom, only moments after I belted wicked little Emily with my perfume-laden pillow.

"Eric, young man!" Mom threatened while squeezing my scrawny little arm. "You should NEVER, and I mean NEVER *hit a girl!*"

"But she called me a Doofhead!" I protested with a face as red as Superman's cape.

"I don't care what she called you! A young man should NEVER *hit a girl!*" With that very clear message reverberating through my cranium, I spent the rest of the day in my room with my perfume-laden pillow and my graffiti-scrawled Bronco's picture. But all was not lost! I learned a valuable chivalrous lesson that miserable day.

As the years passed, I added to my repertoire of "valuable chivalrous lessons." Little blonde Rebecca's blood curdling screams helped teach me *never* to pull the legs off a crawdad in a lady's presence. Then there was Priscilla, the little varmint with red curls from down the street, who helped me understand the virtue of using Lysol to cover guyish fragrances in the "potty room."

By the age of eleven I had learned enough valuable lessons to prevent a girl from fleeing for her life when within a hundred feet of me. But I still had a ways to go when it came to truly romancing a woman.

It didn't come easy, but by the age of twenty I was starting to catch onto this "gentleman" thing. It was Leslie who actually taught me most of what I know when it comes to true chivalrous and romantic goodness.

Rule #1: *Always* and *instantaneously* notice when a woman gets her hair done.

Rule #2: Be a keen observer of how her earrings draw out the sparkle in her lovely eyes.

And finally, Rule #3: Periodically stop at restroom facilities, without being asked, if ever on a trip longer than thirty-seven minutes with a woman in the car.

If young men just put into practice those three things, I think the divorce rate in the next generation of marriages would drop 5 percent. But as a revolutionary romantic, a measly 5 percent doesn't get me excited. I, too, would love to see men begin to sweetly cherish women, and women tenderly honor men the way God designed them to. But just adding a few chivalrous characteristics to our love lives unfortunately won't accomplish *that,* and it certainly won't bring the melody of the "sweeter song" into our romantic relationships.

If we really are after "the beautiful side of love," and the version of romance that would make Hollywood's collective chin drop to the floor, then we need to pursue becoming a lover like the Great Lover Himself! We need to seek to reflect the goodness of our great God. He was not only a Lover who laid down His life for His Bride, and kept Himself spotlessly pure in heart, mind, and body, but He was also a Lover who was wholly faithful. In other words, Jesus knew how to blend his love and purity with patience. He knew how to be single with purpose, in a way that would honor and cherish His future Bride.

If we learn to be a picture of Jesus' faithfulness in how we relate to our future spouse, I guarantee the word "divorce" will become a dusty old term that the up-and-coming generations won't even know how to define.

Becoming a Picture of Jesus

Matt is *finally* married! After over three decades...he's married! Whew! Some guys never marry because they don't want to make a commitment. Then there are those who never "settle down" due to the fact that their breath could knock over a Saint Bernard.

After thirty-two years of singleness, Matt knew it wasn't due to halitosis and it certainly wasn't caused by his inability to commit. You see, Matt's reason for being single had everything to do with a *presence of* commitment. He was committed to a woman whom he had *never met.* And until she came along, he was going to wait, and wait, and wait!

I get tingles when I hear a really good romantic love story. And I got tingles when Matt shared his with me.

My favorite part was right after they had committed to each other to get married and Lisa gazed deeply into his eyes and asked,

"Matthew, will you be faithful to me?"

"Baby Doll," Matt tenderly answered, "I have been faithful to you for thirty-two years!"

Wow! In one moment, because of the commitment he had made in the past, Matt gave his beautiful bride total confidence in the future. Men, your future wife wants to feel that same strength and confidence from you...and you have the power to give it to her. I can hear some of you now: "God, I'm willing to set myself aside completely for my future spouse, but PLEASE DON'T MAKE ME WAIT UNTIL I'M THIRTY-TWO!"

It's an Art

Faithfulness is an attribute of heavenly romance that is extremely misunderstood. How can you be faithful to someone *before* you even meet? Isn't faithfulness a quality that becomes important once a relationship already exists?

Well, just like Norman Rockwell could have never expected to paint a timeless masterpiece if he'd never taken an art lesson in his entire life, neither can you expect to master the art of faithfulness if you wait until the wedding bells chime to start practicing it.

Though only a few can be successful at painting a timeless masterpiece on a canvas, we are *all* commanded by God to be successful in mastering the art of faithfulness. Faithfulness is a discipline that is refined and honed through years of practice. Over time it becomes a habit. In a sense, it is learning to love your future spouse through patiently waiting, consistently hoping, and living by the high standard to which you've been called. I like to picture faithfulness as an oak tree, which patiently endures the torrid winds and rains, only to become stronger and more solid as a result. It is strength learned through persevering; it is integrity gained through waiting. It's imperative to the "beautiful side of love."

Habits

When we are in diapers we begin to establish habit patterns. Breakfast at four in the morning, doo doo at five, temper tantrum at six, bottle at seven, doo doo at eight, hit doggy at nine, doo doo at ten, scribble on wall at eleven, and finally, to cap off the eventful morning, throw squash in Mommy's hair at noon.

As all mommies know, if you are not trained to develop new habits as a toddler, you will not only be an obnoxious adult, but you will still be throwing temper tantrums at the age of twenty-six.

When most of us think of habits, we think of brushing our teeth, locking the front door before going to bed, praying before meals, or my favorite, staring absentmindedly into the refrigerator when I can't remember what it was Leslie asked me to do.

Well, let's expand our horizons a little and invite faithfulness into our definition of habits. Because, not only is faithfulness a bonafide habit, it's the chief habit—both in our love life with our future spouse and in our love life with Jesus, our Great Lover and our King.

Just imagine that inside of your heart there is a place where only one person can ever enter, other than God. It's a combination between a mini-kingdom where you store up your finest treasures, and a dazzling meadow where your sweetest flowers bloom. In this mini-kingdom you store up the most extravagant love, and in this dazzling meadow you nurture your most tender affections. The longer this sanctuary is faithfully guarded, cultivated, and beautified, the more enchanting it will become.

Another Greek Tale

Once upon a time there lived a beautiful queen named Penelope who was carefully weaving a white linen roll. It was to be a gift for her husband whose return she anxiously awaited each day. For years the king had been away in the Trojan War. Each and every day she would say his name over and over again, somehow hoping he would hear the cry of her aching heart.

One day, many great chiefs and princes, all in search of wives, set sail for Ithaca to try to win Penelope's hand. They assured the lonely queen that her husband, the king, had died in battle, and that it would be best for the people of Ithaca and for her own protection that she pick one of them to be her new husband.

But Penelope, with tears in her royal eyes answered, "Heroes and most honored Princes, I refuse to believe what you say. I am certain that my noble husband lives, and I must faithfully keep his kingdom for him till he returns. I am weaving a white linen roll for him even now."

The chiefs and princes stubbornly refused to return home and daily reminded her of her need for a husband and of Ithaca's need for a king.

Weeks passed by, and still Penelope did not bend, but continued to faithfully weave her linen roll in hopes of the king's return. The chiefs and princes tried every possible persuasion, but to no avail. The group of hopeful suitors moved into the palace, drinking the royal wine and consuming the royal food. They refused to depart until Penelope chose one of them to marry.

A weary and reluctant Penelope finally agreed to choose a new husband as soon as she finished weaving her white linen roll, if the king had not returned by then. Weeks passed, and still she kept weaving. However, by night she would secretly unravel all the thread she had woven during the day. Eventually her scheme was discovered.

A leader among them, Agelaus, called the assembly together and addressed Penelope in a loud voice,

"Queen Penelope," he fumed angrily, "your stubbornness has left us no choice but to take this matter into our own hands. We have seen your trickery in delaying the completion of your cursed linen roll, and we will stand for it no longer. Finish it by tomorrow and select your new husband before noon, or we will choose him for you! We will not wait another day!"

The next afternoon all the suitors gathered to await Penelope's royal decision. Just as she entered the banquet hall, a strange beggar quietly crept into the assembly. His tired head was hidden beneath a tattered hood, and a ragged cloak wrapped itself around his decrepit body. He hobbled to the back of the hall quietly, unnoticed save for a few mocking sneers from the suitors he passed. Penelope began to speak, capturing the attention of all present.

"Chiefs and Princes," said Penelope with a knot of grief in her regal throat, "we will leave this decision to fate. Behold, I am holding the great bow of my husband, the king. Each of you must try your strength in bending it, and I will choose the one amongst you who can shoot the most accurate arrow."

"Agreed!" cried the suitors, and they eagerly lined up to test their strength.

One after the other struggled to bend the great bow. Then losing patience, each of the gallant nobles threw it down to the ground and strode away.

"Only a giant could bend that bow of iron!" they moaned.

"Perhaps the filthy old beggar would like to test his strength," one mockingly yelled with a sneer.

At that, the beggar rose from his chair and went with halting steps to the head of the hall.

"You old fool!" the suitors howled in derision as the dirty traveler picked up the great bow.

Suddenly an amazing change came over the stranger. The decrepit traveler straightened his back and rose to his full height, and even in a beggar's rags it was impossible not to notice that this weary traveler was every inch *a king*. Then, without effort, he bent the bow and strung it as everyone in the great hall looked on in astonishment. The king had returned!

The suitors were speechless. Then, in sheer panic, they turned and fled for their lives. But the arrows of the king were swift and accurate, and not a one missed its target. There wasn't a suitor who escaped the vengeance of the king that day.

Penelope ran to her hero, who was clothed in rags, and embraced him. Then, with the voice of an angel she said, "I have faithfully kept your kingdom, my noble king!" She tenderly presented him with a soft white linen roll. "I have spent years weaving this gift in hopes of your return. On the day I finished it, I was told to choose a husband." Then, placing a tender kiss upon his soiled cheek, she said, "And I choose *you*."[1]

A Hurried Generation

Isn't faithfulness heroic? Too bad our society doesn't honor it like it used to. If Penelope were a typical nineties woman she would have run off with the first cute prince who stepped foot on her shore. But instead, she seemed to understand what it means to guard a kingdom, and to tearfully wait for her lover.

In our microwavable-fast food generation, all our desires can be met with the click of a button. Telling you to *wait* and actually having you listen, is just as likely as my throwing a side of beef to a ravenous lion and telling him to put it in a Tupperware container and save it for tomorrow. We are use to getting everything we want *now*, and to be honest, we don't want to wait.

In fact, our generation is suffering from a mental disease that my good friend Dave calls, the "let-me-laugh-now-and-I'll-do-my-crying-later-if-I'm-still-alive" syndrome. In other words, most of us don't think about our future and how our decisions today will effect us over the long haul.

I honestly never thought I would live past the age of twenty-five. Why? I don't quite know, but maybe it had something to do with the fact that I was told over three thousand seven hundred and nine times that the end of the world was upon us. When sun tanning on the beach, I drenched myself in baby oil because I just knew I wouldn't be around to suffer the consequences of skin cancer. When heating up macaroni and cheese, I would stare into the microwave like a peeping Tom because I was certain I wouldn't be around to suffer the consequences of a warped and radiated brain. And in relationships, I would do things physically with my date that I knew were dishonoring to my future spouse because I was certain I wouldn't get married before the end of the world came.

It's no wonder they smack an "X" on our generation. We are known as "the generation without purpose and without hope." And as some have even entitled us, "the first generation to live after the death of God." Here we are searching for something "beautiful," yet the whole source of that beautiful has been robbed from us. The amazing and romantic world around us is explained away as a freak act of nature, our dearest friends are really only a heap of meaningless matter who evolved from a puddle of sludge. And *love itself* is but a chemical reaction inside our brains that takes place when our impulse to *propagate our species* kicks into gear.

To be honest, if modern science is right and all that exists is nothing but the result of a great "Big Bang," then I would be the first one to say that you are crazy if you *wait* to indulge your desires. I mean, if you and the "love of your life" are only heaps of meaningless matter, then hurry up and get that chemical reaction ignited!

We as a generation have become experts in the *biology,* but we are illiterate when it comes to the *"beautiful."* We are tirelessly in search of it, but we will never find it until we realize that the "beautiful" *is God!* No matter how many times we have sex, no matter how many times we hear the words "I love you," it will forever be empty if we don't blend it with the God who invented true love and is Himself the Author of Romance. When you take God out of the center of your world, everything sweet, tender, pure, and lovely is sure to quickly follow.

A Voice Crying in the Wilderness

We have been trained to be in a hurry. We pace in front of microwaves, we complain of slow service at drive-through windows, and we tap our foot impatiently for the elevator to finally arrive at the third floor. But, in our minds, it's all for a good reason. We believe deep down inside that it's all coming to an end soon, and our time to indulge ourselves is growing increasingly less, every day, every minute!

I must sound a bit like John the Baptist with a leopard carcass wrapped around my wiry body and an unkempt beard growing every-which-way, as I cry in the wilderness, "Hey everyone! Learn to be patient!"

I have gained a deep respect for the Beatles' original promoter. In 1962, Decca Recording Company turned them down saying,

"We don't like their sound. Groups of guitars are on their way out."

But little did Decca know what an incredible sound they were passing up! It's even more difficult being a promoter of Truth in 1999, hearing how "all that Jesus stuff is on the way out!" No offense to all of you Beatles' fans out there, but *Hey Jude* is like a horribly warbled note played on a tin can in a junk yard next to the amazingly sweet song Jesus wants to play in each of our lives.

Jesus teaches a message of purposeful patience and a message of dazzling faithfulness. It's a message that says,

Be still, and know that I am God.

Psalm 46:10 NIV

In repentance and rest is your salvation, in quietness and trust is your strength.

Isaiah 30:15 NIV

In His ever-gentle way He wants to lift us up on His lap, wrap His big strong arms around us, wipe away our tears of longing and pain, and whisper in our ears,

"It's all right, little child. Just rest your head on My shoulder. I will take care of you. This world is always in a hurry, but I teach My children patience. Live, expecting a full and joyous life. And learn to trust My perfect timing so that you may discover that all the pain found in waiting has a magnificent and awesome purpose."

Lonely Rainy Nights

Patience is more than endurance. A saint's life is in the hands of God like a bow and arrow in the hands of an archer. God is aiming at something the saint cannot see, and He stretches and strains, and every now and again the saint says—"I cannot stand any more." God does not heed, He goes on stretching till His purpose is in sight, then He lets fly. Trust yourself in God's hands. Maintain your relationship to Jesus Christ by the patience of faith. "Though He slay me, yet will I wait for Him."[2]

Oswald Chambers

I vividly remember a lonely rainy night in 1991. I was single and not very happy about it. In fact, the pulsating desire I had to share my life with a young woman was overwhelming. I tried to pray, but all I could do was groan. I didn't know Leslie yet, and, to be honest, I was starting to doubt that a future spouse for me even existed. I wrestled with God, sub-consciously grabbing for the "pen" I had entrusted to Him a year earlier. If God was going to script my love story, I thought *now* would be a good time to at least let me know He had picked the characters for the drama.

I like to call them "God moments." If you have ever had one, you will know exactly what I mean. He is always with us, but in a "God moment" He is there with us in an intimate and life-changing way. Just as seeing the Colorado Rocky Mountains on a map doesn't compare to seeing their awesome majesty in person, so knowing that God is *there* through academic reason, doesn't compare to knowing that God is *there* through a "God moment."

In a "God moment" God's Word is living; it's not just literature packaged nicely inside the cover of your Bible. And in a "God moment" Jesus is alive and powerful, not just a great historical figure stowed away in the antiquated annals of the past.

It was on this lonely rainy night in 1991, right smack in the middle of my pity party, that I had a "God moment."

I was in my room on my knees groaning, when God poured His version of Tabasco into my heart. I remember my heart burning with the realization of how enormous, how powerful, how capable, how merciful, how tender, and how loving God is. I remember realizing, once again, how ridiculous it was for me *not* to put my complete trust in *His* way of doing things. And I remember weeping with my hands over my face as I once again told God, "I'm willing to wait, Lord Jesus!"

I picked up a pen and pulled a piece of notebook paper out of my desk drawer and began to write. With tears still dribbling down my cheeks, I was determined to somehow tell my wife-to-be, wherever she was, that I was waiting just for her! I wrote,

I feel the rain tap on my head,
Could it be your tears? Do you need a friend?

I don't know how far, and I don't know how long,
All I know is that He's faithful.
Such a love, it burns deep inside
I know that you'll be worth all the tears that I
have cried.

Years later, I pulled those simplistic words from my journal and sat down at the piano, but this time I wasn't alone. I tearfully sang to my brand new wife the words that were crafted just for her amid my lonely rainy night of pain-filled waiting.

Pulling a Penelope

The sweetest things in this world today have come to us through tears and pain.[3]

J. R. Miller

All of you in our generation, listen up! Let's pull a Penelope. All the chiefs and princes of the land are trying to convince us that we need to settle for less, and that our hopes and dreams are unrealistic and ridiculous. But let's be faithful despite all the talk; let's patiently endure despite the fact that days, weeks, months, even years are passing by and there is still no word from our lover. Let's pull a Penelope and bring heroism back to our generation. Let's pull a Penelope and discover the stupendous and marvelous reward to patience. Let's pull a Penelope and endure the great pain, to find the great gain.

Each of us has lonely rainy days in our life. But very few of us know how to turn our cloudy days into a beautiful tomorrow. One of my favorite, little corny sayings comes from an anniversary card Leslie and I once received. It says,

"When two people really, really love each other, even rainy days are fun!"

That can be true *before* marriage just as it can be true after those wedding bells ring. When you find yourself alone on a rainy day, pull a Penelope, and weave for your future lover your own version of a "white linen roll."

Most people never realize that loneliness is a gift from God. Not only can it draw us closer to Jesus, it can teach us to cherish a long awaited marriage relationship all the more. And in that loneliness, we can weave a gift of our own for the person who will make all our faithful waiting worthwhile someday. Learn to pray for them on those rainy days, asking God to mold them into the perfect compliment to your life. Write love letters to them. Just think, you can invite them into the deepest caverns of your heart and let them take a peek inside the days, months, even years of your life that they will not have had the privilege of sharing *except* through your writing. If you are musical, write a love song. If you're an artist, paint a picture. And if you're a woodworker, carve for them something that will let them forever know that they were "worth the wait!"

Believe it or not, Penelope wasn't the first to "pull a Penelope." God invented the concept of faithfulness before the beginning of time. He was the ultimate model of pain-filled patience and purposeful waiting. With tears in His tender eyes, *even now* He waits for some of us to finally let Him have His way in our life. When you finally arrive at His open palace gate, He will run to you and embrace you, and whisper in your ear,

"You, my child, were worth the pain-filled wait!"

A Step Further

In our culture, we think it is hard to wait for two months, but try thousands of years. Turn to Luke 2:21-40 and find a truly amazing example of faithfulness. It is the story of a nation, but more specifically, of a man and a woman who spent their life waiting, and how God truly honored them for it. After you finish reading, ask yourself the question, "If I knew it would bless God's heart, would I be willing to wait for my spouse with the same faithfulness and expectancy that this godly man and woman had?"

Chapter Ten

Leslie:
Can the Sweeter
Song Be a Solo?

*Understanding the pain
and purpose of singleness*

Honeymoon Love Letters

Eric's face was alight with boyish excitement as he reached into his suitcase and pulled out a huge spiral notebook.

"I have something I want to show you, Les," he said softly, a smile playing on his lips.

It was our honeymoon—by far the most incredible two weeks of my life. After waiting for what had seemed like an eternity, I was finally *Mrs. Eric Ludy!* And just when I thought I had discovered the depth of Eric's love for me, he took it to yet a deeper level.

"See all these letters?" he said, flipping through page after page of notebook paper. "I wrote these to you years before we ever met. I've been saving them for our honeymoon!"

For hours, I poured through the letters, fascinated by this man I had married. I was intrigued by his amazing journey as a single person, before I had known him.

"Tonight I am on a mission trip in Bulgaria," wrote one, "and I long for you to be with me in the joy of ministering God's truth."

"I am gazing at a gorgeous sunset," said another, "and it's not the same without you here to share it. I don't know where you are tonight, but I'm praying for you. I love you."

Though the letters were not addressed to me, they may as well have had my name on them. Each one, in its unique way, told of Eric's unfailing love and devotion to the woman who would one day share his life with him. His faithfulness to me before we met gave me such security in our marriage. As I read the letters, I felt more like a princess than I ever had. What an honor to be chosen by God to be that special woman to love this man for a lifetime!

It may seem strange that I would begin a chapter on singleness with a story of my incredible honeymoon. No, I am not trying to torture you singles! The point is, this is not just a chapter about being single. This is a chapter about being single *with a purpose*. Whenever God takes us through a challenging time, we can endure the pain if we cling to the hope that in the end we will discover that it was all for a purpose. We can know that someday it will all be worth it. Whether your singleness ends with a romantic dream come true here on this earth, or a glorious celebration in eternity, God *does* have an ultimate purpose in mind for this solo season of your life.

I know that day when Eric saw his new wife reading love letters he had written to her years earlier, he must have said to himself, "This was worth all those years of waiting. This was worth all those lonely rainy nights." And one day you, too, will be able to echo his words.

Creative Singleness

Jean and Kirsty are two bright young women from the "land down under." Jean, a recent college graduate and new art teacher, and Kirsty, a policewoman in training, have been best friends for many years. Their fun-loving personalities and unmistakable Australian accents make them two very entertaining people to converse with. During their recent visit to America, Eric and I talked with them both in depth about their journeys as single women.

"God has really made it clear to me that the reason I still haven't found the right guy is because He's not finished preparing me for marriage," Jean told us in her cute, cuddly voice. "Right now I'm just learning to be God's princess. He is showing me that I am *enough,* as I am, even if I never get married."

Is it easy? Not at all. As Kirsty put it, "I dream of the man I'm going to marry all the time. Jean and I like to imagine what type of guys we are waiting for. We talk about the most important character qualities we want our future husbands to have. But sometimes it gets so disheartening. There just don't seem to be too many men with real integrity! It's easy to feel like we're waiting for something that doesn't exist."

In addition to the problem of not seeing available godly men anywhere in sight, another issue we girls have had to face is disapproval from others.

"We've been told that our standards are too high. We've been told that we'll never get married if we don't go out there, meet men, and make ourselves available," Jean said with discouragement in her eyes.

But Jean and Kirsty have remained steadfast, waiting for God to write a love story for each of them, if He should choose to, in His perfect time. And they've even had fun with their commitment to wait!

"Every Valentine's Day, instead of letting ourselves be all depressed because we're single, we make valentine love letters for our future husbands," Kirsty told us with joy on her pretty face. "We have a great time doing it, and it reminds us that this season of our life has a purpose. We save all these letters to give to our husbands someday."

Now *that's* creative singleness! Jean and Kirsty's journey of pain mixed with hope is the essence of what singleness is all about. It's not easy. But it has a profound purpose. And someday, with love in His gentle eyes, their Lord will reward them for their faithfulness. In that moment, it will be worth it all for Jean and Kirsty.

Radiant Singleness

"If I hear one more married person preach about singleness being a gift, I'm going to gag!" declared Brice, a twenty-eight-year-old single we met at a speaking event in Texas, who is more than ready for marriage. "Married people forget what it's like to be alone!"

Maybe married people don't forget—they just block out the memory of singleness because they don't want to relive it! Singleness is a lonely path. But does it have to be a form of hell on earth?

Brice has lived the past eight years of his life in misery. He is obsessed with finding the right girl and finally shedding the "curse" of singleness. In many ways, he has put his life on hold until the issue of getting married is resolved. He hasn't pursued finding out his life's calling or goals because he feels incomplete. He hasn't grown spiritually and he hasn't prepared practically; he has just angrily cried out to God to send a wife to him ASAP! Brice has grown bitter and resentful. His greatest fear is dying before he finds someone to love.

Brice represents the plight of many singles in today's culture. As a Christian community, we have not acknowledged God's purpose for the season of singleness, which is causing singles to feel devalued or lesser-than.

Jen, a fun-loving and deeply spiritually senior in college, says that it seems everywhere she goes she is asked the same question, "So, are you dating anyone?"

"It's really hard to hear that question over and over," admits Jen, "because there is so much more to who I am than a relationship. I have school, ministry, and, most importantly, my relationship with the Lord. I hardly ever get asked about those other areas of my life, and if I do, it's only secondary to people wanting to find out about the relationship area. When the focus is so much on the relationship area, it's easy to start thinking that you need to have a relationship to be considered a "whole person." But that's not true. I am a whole person right now, even in this season of singleness."

The fact that Jen understands there is so much more to her life than just finding a relationship is truly amazing in a culture that puts so much emphasis on the importance of pairing up with someone. She has had just as much indirect pressure from Christians in her life to "find someone" as from non-Christians. She feels a lack of support from the Body of Christ in her commitment to trust God for her future spouse.

And countless other young women are "just waiting around" for their future spouse. They don't feel their life can really begin until they are married.

A joke often heard on college campuses is the saying, "Oh, she's here to go after a "M-r-s. degree." In other words, she could care less about college; she just wants to find a husband!

In spite of the temptation to wait for life to begin until after we find that special someone, there *is* more God has for us during a season of singleness than just learning the art of misery and impatience.

Krissy, my beautiful sister-in-law, is thirty-one and still single. She is the best example of purposeful singleness I have ever seen. When she was a teenager, Krissy made a choice to remain faithful to her future husband and to wait for him patiently until God chooses to bring him into her life. That was nearly eighteen years ago. Has Krissy's life been on hold since then? Quite the opposite. Krissy is not just content in her singleness...she is *radiant* in her singleness. Not that she is just tickled pink about being single. But she sees this season of her life as nothing less than a precious gift from God. She understands her singleness to be part of the ultimate plan for her life from her loving Creator.

In the past eighteen years, Krissy has devoted herself completely to the Lord. It is evident to everyone who knows her that she is passionately in love with Jesus Christ. She is joyful, fun-loving, and excited about living. She has been able to develop her God-given talents as a teacher, counselor, artist, and writer. She has energetically poured herself into serving others and enjoying friendships of all ages. Her life is indeed full.

When asked by her younger brother, Marky, one day, "Krissy, do you think you are called to singleness?" she paused, reflected a moment, then replied, "Today I am."

Wow! What a response! *Today I am.* Krissy doesn't see her singleness as an unending hill to climb. She allows God to lead her through this journey *one day at a time.* And as a result, she has discovered a joy in this season that few singles realize they can find.

It hasn't been easy for Krissy. She, like most other singles, has experienced many nights full of painful, lonely tears. She has felt the unquenchable longing for companionship, the agonizing ache for true love. But in those times, she has leaned all the harder upon her Savior. And He has been faithful each step of the way.

Not without design does God write the music of our lives. Be it ours to learn the tune, and not be dismayed at the "rests." They are not to be slurred over, not to be omitted, not to destroy the melody, not to change the keynote. If we look up, God Himself will beat the time for us. With the eye on Him, we shall strike the next note full and clear.

If we sadly say to ourselves, "There is no music in a 'rest,'" let us not forget "there is the making of music in it." The making of music is often a slow and painful process in this life. How patiently God works to teach us!

How long He waits for us to learn the lesson![1]

Ruskin

Productive Singleness

When we, like Krissy, are willing to allow God to use this season of our lives for *His purposes,* we discover an incredible truth: Singleness doesn't have to be a time of passive and futile waiting. Instead it can be an exciting adventure of active preparation. Let's look at some of the ways God may be using singleness to mold us into His likeness and prepare us for a future relationship.

1. Singleness can strengthen our inward character qualities.

Godly Contentment

I remember learning a great lesson from the movie *Cool Runnings.* It's a story about a young Jamaican athlete who has a life-long dream of winning a gold medal at the Olympics. After a series of events, he finally makes it to the Olympics, his heart set on winning. But just before the competition, his coach gives him an important piece of advice. "Listen, kid. A gold medal is a wonderful thing. But if you aren't enough *without it,* believe me, you'll never be enough *with it.*"

Tyler, a twenty-five-year-old single musician, points out that the biggest struggle most singles seem to have, himself included, is assuming that once a relationship comes into your life it will make everything perfect.

"I don't want to put off living," he told us with sincerity in his baby-blue eyes. "My life doesn't start once I finally get married—my life has already started. I want to soak up every day for all it's worth, not just wait around for things to be perfect. I want to enjoy each year of my life to the fullest."

A relationship is not meant to make us into a whole person—only Jesus Christ can make us a whole person. Marriage should never become that gold medal we strive for that will finally make us "enough." We must learn to be "enough" right now, just as we are, in Christ alone.

While getting married someday may bring us great joy, we truly do have a reason to be happy and content no matter what season of life we are in—because of what Jesus Christ has done for us. True contentment can only be found in an intimate love relationship with the Lord, not in anything else, *including* a romantic love story. Singleness can teach us this contentment. In this season we can learn what is means to have peace and joy in Christ, no matter what our circumstances may be. And in a culture that is always longing for something more, "But godliness with contentment is great gain" (1 Tim. 6:6 NIV).

Gaining the Strength to Stand Alone

Sometime ago Elisabeth Elliot make this profound statement: *"Loneliness is a required course for leadership."*[2]

During a time when I was single, I felt completely alone—away from friends and family, away from Eric, away from anyone who really knew me—these simple words gave me perspective on the purpose for my loneliness. God was using the loneliness to teach me complete dependence upon Him. I could no longer look to other people for my confidence. I had no choice but to find my courage and hope in Him. This kind of total dependence on the Lord was preparing me to become more effective for His kingdom. I was gaining the inward strength of character I would need to become a leader for Him.

A true leader must have enough backbone to stand alone—even when the crowd wants to take the easy road home. A true leader cannot be dependent on companionship for his or her security, but must learn to trust in God alone. Singleness can give us this kind of backbone—courage, confidence, and leadership skills that any effective Christian must learn.

Discovering His Gentle Arms of Love

Many years ago Amy Grant used to sing, "I love a lonely day...it chases me to You."[3]

Years later I often heard those words echoing back through my mind during times of feeling alone. We can let the inward ache drive us into His ready arms, or simply try to bear it alone in agony.

Eric went through a time of profound loneliness while he was taking a semester off from college. He had just come from a busy schedule at school that included sports, study, and an active social life. He had been surrounded constantly by his good friends. But now, back at home with an empty schedule, while all his buddies were still at school and his family was occupied with their own lives, he felt an intense inward pain as he'd never before known. One day he found himself on his knees, weeping into the fabric of the sofa. The loneliness had become too much to handle. As he cried out to his Lord, he suddenly felt a tremendous peace wash over him. It was almost as if Jesus Himself were kneeling beside Eric, wrapping a tender arm around his shoulder and whispering words of love and comfort to his soul.

That afternoon Eric sat at the piano and wrote the lyrics to what is one of our favorite songs to this day...

> *I am like a deer, You are like the water*
> *I run to You, like a son to his Father*
> *I felt so alone, like a moth without a flame*
> *But You ignited, and to You I came*
> *And that's forever.*

I felt so alone like a ship without a sea
But You gave me water, You took my hand and
said to me
"This is for eternity."

I'll never be lonely
I'll never be lonely with You
I've got this feeling that You're here to stay
And I know I'll never be lonely with You.

It's so exciting to know that though we may be singing a solo in life, we are never truly alone! Singleness is an opportunity to allow Christ's gentle arms to encircle our hearts and discover how very much He loves us.

2. Singleness allows time to focus on practical preparation.

Discovering and Developing Talents and Life Skills

God has created us each with unique gifts, abilities, and heart desires. He has a master plan for each of our lives. Singleness is a time to seek Him with an undivided, undistracted heart. When a relationship comes into our life, often who we are as an individual gets swallowed up, and our identity becomes wrapped up in that other person. Being single is an opportunity to discover who God has made us to be and what He has called us to in this life.

Before Eric and I started our relationship, I went through a time where it seemed that opportunities for me to minister to young women were flooding into my life. As a single person, I had the time and energy to focus on this "informal" ministry. I loved every minute spending time with these girls. I spent hours responding to letters, taking them out to lunch, or seeking to encourage them over the phone. I realized through this experience that the Lord was showing me one of the forms of ministry for which He had created me. If I had been in a relationship, focused entirely on getting married, most likely I wouldn't have had the time or energy to discover or pursue this call in my life. The skills I developed during that time helped prepare me for the ministry God later called Eric and me to as a team.

Ann, from chapter 8, is using this season of singleness to hone her natural talents and God-given desires. She has been able to grow in areas such as music, writing, and public speaking skills.

"With a relationship in my life," she told me, "I would probably never be able to give these areas the time and attention needed to really blossom them into useful skills. I value the chance to focus on pursuing these desires."

One of my closest friends is Molly, a bubbly attractive blonde with a great sense of humor. At twenty-one, she is using this season of solo in her life to broaden her horizons with things she's always wanted to do. During the week, she works for a corporation as an administrative assistant. In her free time, she is studying voice and developing her skills as a musician. She is also taking time to serve others.

"I may never be this free in my life again," she reasons, "so I want to use it to bless others as much as possible."

Molly took a counselor's training course at her local crisis pregnancy center and now volunteers weekly as a counselor to the center's clients.

Kyle, a twenty-two-year-old single from New Zealand, is using this time in his life to experience the mission field through short-term mission trips. He has been to several countries to serve needy people and share the Gospel. It's an experience that has changed his life, broadened his horizons, led him closer to the Lord, and helped him discover the areas where he is most gifted. He is learning how to use his unique gifts for God's glory.

What are the desires of *your* heart? To train as a musician or athlete? To pursue a college education? To backpack across the country? To go into missionary work? Maybe it's even to simply spend a season at home serving your own family and community in practical ways. Singleness can be the perfect time for developing life skills and discovering how to use your talents for the Lord.

Back to the Basics

Before Eric came into my life, I had to go through a time of practical preparation for married life. As silly as it seems, I had gone through most of my youth without learning how to keep a budget, balance a checkbook, pay bills, or even cook real food that was not from a can or box. I had been too pre-occupied with my social life and school to focus on tasks that didn't really affect my life at the time. Now God wanted to prepare me in some of the most basic areas I had missed, *before* He brought a man into my life and things would drastically change. For about a year, my focus became practical preparation in basic life skills. And believe me, Eric is now quite appreciative that I learned those things!

Being married in the real world takes teamwork. If we are of the mindset that we are going to rely on our spouse to do all the practical work of living a responsible adult life, we are in for trouble.

I know many young men who have mothers who always cooked for them, made their beds, and did their laundry until the day they left home. These young men never learned even the most elementary aspects of keeping house. One of two scenarios usually takes place in these unfortunate men's lives. The first option is that they become bachelors with homes that need to be quarantined by the local government health department. The second possibility is that they get married and drive their poor wives to the brink of insanity by leaving a trail of dirty socks, dishes, and open-toilet-seats wherever they go, expecting her to "take care of it." Needless to say, the first option doesn't add to the aura of desirability of a bachelor looking for love, and the second scenario causes some fairly colorful conflicts between a husband and wife!

Guys, take a little advice and use this time of singleness to prepare in practical ways for managing a home. The woman you marry will love you for it, and you will significantly reduce the amount of "nagging" you are subject to during your married lifetime!

Eric, my noble knight, is usually the one who cleans the bathroom in our house (something I can't stand doing). Whenever he selflessly scrubs the toilet without complaining, I am reminded once again how blessed I am to have a man like him. This may not sound romantic, but to me it is *very* romantic! Eric displays his undying love for me when he gives of himself in these simple, basic ways.

This advice isn't just for guys. It's for everyone. My goal is to serve Eric in everyday life, just like he serves me. While he cleans the bathroom, I do the laundry, which is the one thing *he* can't stand. This kind of teamwork is something both men and women can plan and prepare for long before marriage.

Only *you* can know what practical areas in *your* life need some work. Maybe it's not housework, but learning how to budget and keep track of finances. Maybe it's learning how to grocery shop and prepare meals. Pray that God will give you the discipline to develop and strengthen these important basic skills. It may not seem very romantic, but there are few more practical ways to put selfless love into practice! And besides, think of what a hindrance smelly socks and dirty dishes are to a lovely candlelit dinner!

Marriage Is for Everyone

"But why should I bother with preparation for marriage if God never wants me to be married at all?" asked Carl, a frustrated single from Michigan with no prospect of finding a bride in the near future.

In truth, most of us *will* be married in our lifetime. It only makes sense that we should plan and prepare accordingly. But even if God has chosen a lifetime of singleness for us, we will still experience a marriage someday. When Christ, our true Bridegroom, appears in all His glory, He will come for His Bride, the church. In actuality, heaven is going to be one huge marriage celebration which all believers will be a part of for all eternity. Marriage between a man and woman here on this earth should be a glimpse of the beauty of the ultimate marriage that is to come. Whether or not we experience an earthly marriage, we can all prepare and make ready for our true Bridegroom. (Yes, men, this does apply to you as well! If it sounds wimpy to think of yourself as being the "Bride" of Christ, don't worry, in heaven it won't be!)

Final Countdown

One of the best lessons Eric and I learned about preparing for our true Bridegroom happened just before our wedding. The longer we were engaged, the more intense our longing grew to finally be together. About two months before the wedding, we half-jokingly thought about eloping just to put ourselves out of the misery. However, we both knew that it would be worth waiting till the proper time. And plus, it had taken me hours to find the perfect wedding dress! I was not going to miss my big day to shine!

So, we stuck it out. Eric was teaching in Michigan, while I was doing secretarial work and planning the wedding in Colorado. We racked up quite a phone bill over those few months! I was constantly calling to remind him to make hotel reservations, invite relatives to the rehearsal dinner, and go get sized for a tux. Like a true bachelor, he waited until the last possible day to accomplish all of these tasks, but he did get them done, thankfully. And finally it was down to the final week before our wedding. Two days before Eric hopped a flight to Colorado to get married, he had to teach one last day of

Constitutional Law to his students. Needless to say, his mind was anywhere but on the five key elements to the Preamble!

"All I could think about was Leslie, Leslie, Leslie," he said later. "My vocabulary had been reduced to one word...Leslie! I couldn't teach, I couldn't carry on a normal conversation with anyone, I couldn't even pray!"

The last day of teaching government, Eric made up a creative game for his students to play since his mind was mush anyway. Any guesses what the name of his game was? That's right...L-e-s-l-i-e! What else would it be? In case you were wondering, it had nothing to do with Constitutional Law.

For four hours he forced his poor students to play "L-e-s-l-i-e." They were probably running for the door when class was finally dismissed, convinced that their lovesick teacher had finally snapped. But Eric didn't care. He was so excited to be married...nothing else mattered.

Back in Colorado, I was feeling the same way. The anticipation of wearing my dress and walking down the aisle was nothing compared to the longing I had to finally become Mrs. Eric Ludy...to be with the man I loved forever.

And that's when we realized a profound truth. This longing to be with the one we loved was precisely the longing we should have to be with our Lord, our true Bridegroom, for all eternity.

Desiderio Domini

Nearly all God's jewels are crystallized tears.[4]

Mrs. Charles Cowman

There is an ancient story passed down through generations of Christians about the apostle Peter during the latter years of his life. It was said that he would often weep whenever a cock would crow. Of course, if we know Bible history, we understand why. But it was also said that Peter would often weep at other times, and no one quite knew the reason.

Finally one day, a young saint worked up enough courage to ask him about it.

"Peter, why do you so often weep?" he inquired cautiously.

Peter turned to the young man, and with a look of intense yearning burning in his eyes he replied softly, "Desiderio Domini."

Translated from Latin into modern day English, "Desiderio Domini" means, "I dearly long to be with my Lord."

Peter had spent his time among men. Now he was ready for heaven, with a longing that grew stronger each and every day to be able to run into the loving arms of his dearest friend and Savior, Jesus Christ.

Growing up in the church, Eric and I both had always thought of the "last days" before Christ comes back as a time of great fear and turmoil for Christians. But in thinking it through, we realized that the last days are merely the final countdown before the great wedding celebration in heaven. It's a time of great anticipation and excitement! We, as the Bride of Christ, should be absolutely consumed, not by fear, but by joy, knowing that soon we will be with Him forever and all our longings will be satisfied.

Whether single or married on this earth, our heart's longing and our first love should be for the One who gave everything for us, who is preparing a place for us in heaven, and who is returning again soon for His Bride.

A Step Further

Sneak off to a quiet place. Bring your Bible, a piece of paper, and a pen. Turn to the book of John and read chapter 12, verses 1 through 8. It is the story of someone who knew how to use her singleness to bless the heart of God. After you read this touching story, write a love note to Jesus, pour out the worshipful perfume of your heart. Tell Him how much you need Him to fill that aching void in your heart for a lover.

Chapter Eleven

Leslie:
Holding Out for a Higher Standard

*Do noble knights and
fair maidens really exist?*

My Perfect Prince

He was tall, muscle-bound and incredibly good-looking. His sandy-blonde hair had a wind-blown outdoorsy look and perfectly complemented his bronzed skin. His bright blue eyes sparkled at all times, and whenever he smiled the dimple on his chin stood out in the most adorable way.

He was a perfect gentleman. He was charming, amazingly sensitive, brave, bold, gentle, and tender. Whenever a lady was in distress, he seemed to intrinsically know it. He would hurriedly zip up his rugged leather bomber jacket and dash to the rescue just in the nick of time. Once he even saved a fair maiden from a life of oppression by vanquishing her persecutors and carrying her back to live happily ever after at his mansion, which was so dazzling and luxurious that most referred to it as a literal castle. Did I forget to mention that he was also rich?

Any female reader who has just perused this man's immaculate description has one important question burning upon her heart—*who is he, and can I have his phone number?*

Well, I can tell you who he is, but I cannot give you his phone number, because you see, he isn't real.

I thought he sounded too good to be true! I can just hear all the ladies grumble.

That's exactly what *I* said to myself a few years ago. All my life I'd dreamed of "him." He was the ideal man. Maybe it came from an overdose of Barbie and Cinderella when I was young. I always imagined that the guy I would marry was going to be a perfect blend of Prince Charming from Cinderella, (*or* he could be the Prince Charming from Snow White—I think they might possibly be the same guy), and "Ken" (you know, from Ken and Barbie).

At any rate, my standards were just a *little* high when I entered the dating world. I was always on the lookout for this man of my dreams. I had no doubt that he would show himself soon and carry me away to his castle.

This presented a problem. You see, not only were there absolutely *no* guys that fit "his" description, but the young men in my life seemed to be the exact *opposite* of what I was looking for! I was looking for a gorgeous knight in shining armor, and all I saw around me were a bunch of immature Brad-Pitt-wanna-be's who were egotistical, selfish, hormone-crazed, and sadly lacking in the "gentlemanly" department!

One of my first wake-up calls came from an experience I had when I was only fourteen. I was talking on the phone with one of my "studly" guy friends one night. After about an hour of discussing meaningless topics such as math homework, rock bands, and movies, we ran out of things to say. There was an unspoken rule between fourteen-year-olds that you had to get in at least five hours of phone talking each night. I was still about two hours short of quota, and so was he. Hanging up the phone and doing our homework was simply not an option. We pondered what to do about our dilemma. Finally he had a brainstorm.

"I know!" he said excitedly, "Brandon is over at Trevor's house right now. Let me call them up on three-way and I won't tell them you are listening in. Then you can hear what a guy conversation sounds like when girls aren't around!"

I suppose that when I was fourteen you could have classified me as a ditz. Naively, I thought his idea was brilliant and waited enthusiastically while he dialed up the numbers of two of his friends. Within moments, the three of them were bantering back and forth in their puberty-stricken monotones, the way only teenage guys can. At first I was bored with their discussion about weight-lifting and trying out for the basketball team, but then they moved on to a topic that instantly caught my attention...girls!

I held my breath as I waited for them to reveal their true feelings about the girls with whom they were currently in love. But the words they spoke were *not* what I was expecting. They began describing, in colorful detail, exactly what they liked about the bodies of girls from school—many of the girls they mentioned were my friends. They talked about the female anatomy as if girls were nothing more than pieces of meat to devour! I was shocked! Their language was so graphic that the conversation sounded like I'd just called a 900-porn number! I felt disgusted and horrified!

When my guy friend finally hung up with his buddies (guy conversations never seem to last as long as girls') he asked me, "So what did you think of that?"

"Is that *really* how guys talk about girls?" I breathed incredulously.

"Sure. What's wrong with it?" he replied flippantly.

"So guys basically see girls as *sex objects?*" I questioned as my voice rose an octave higher.

"Well, sortof, yeah," was his brutally honest response.

That was my first indication that finding a knight in shining armor was not going to be as easy as I had always imagined. As I grew older I began to make the observation that if I was ever going to have normal dating relationships, I was going to *have* to lower my standards in what I wanted in a guy. I went from dreaming of a noble Prince Charming to settling for anyone who didn't seem to think of me as a mere sex object.

Long before I reached the age of twenty-one I had come to a painful conclusion...*most guys are jerks!* I have declared that very observation to many audiences, and it usually brings me a few angry glares from the men present, and a rousing applause from all females within earshot!

Most guys *are* jerks in today's perverted and warped culture. It is sad, but true.

It's more common for men to follow in the footsteps of Eric's locker-room buddy Donny Lucero, than for them to aspire to become a gallant knight.

I wrote previously that I came to a point in my life where I made the decision to save my treasure of purity both inward and outward for my future husband. It was a difficult choice that caused me to change my lifestyle in such a radical way. Though I was seeking to honor the man I would one day marry, sometimes it felt useless. What was the point of aspiring to the "sweeter song," of trusting God for a beautiful romance, of setting myself aside in selfless love for my future spouse, *if men worth waiting for don't even exist?*

I know that question is not just something *I* asked. Everywhere I travel it seems I meet beautiful, godly young women who are wondering whether there is really a knight in shining armor somewhere out there for them. They can't see any eligible men in their life that would warrant the pain and sacrifice of waiting for the "beautiful side of love." There seems to be a worldwide shortage of "real men!"

I remember having a conversation with a friend of mine who had been married to a wonderful Christian man for five years. "I don't know if my standards are too high," I told her, "I am so confused. I have all these desires for a certain type of man, but I haven't even seen one guy who fits what I'm longing for in a husband!"

Her advice that day has stayed with me for years. She reminded me of the promise God gave in Psalm 37:4 (NIV):

> *Delight yourself in the Lord, and He will give you the desires of your heart.*

"Leslie, what are the main qualities you've always wanted in a man?" she asked.

I thought for a moment, then whipped out my mental checklist that I'd tucked away in a corner of my mind, adding to it over the years. "Well, I want someone who treats me like a princess, someone who is sensitive, tender, gentle, brave, full of integrity, servant-hearted, and honorable just to name a few," I answered. Then I laughed self-consciously. "I guess I'm holding out for Prince Charming," I said sheepishly.

"Not really," she replied. "Just think about all those qualities you mentioned. Who can you think of that is the *perfect example* of all those character traits?"

"Uh...Superman?" I guessed. (Well, Clark Kent *is* sort of a Ken-look-alike!)

"No. Jesus Christ," she responded, eyes shining. "You see Leslie, those desires for that kind of a man have been in your heart from a young age. But you are not the one who came up with those longings. It was God who put them in your heart...because He wants you to look for a man *with the character of Jesus Christ.*"

Wow! What a truth! *God* had given me the desire for a godly, Christlike man, because that's exactly the type of man He wanted to bring me! It wasn't that I was supposed to hold out for a man who never made mistakes and was absolutely perfect in every way. Maybe my childhood imaginations *had* been a bit larger than life. But in no way did God want me to settle for one of the typical "jerks" who were a dime-a-dozen. He wanted me to save myself for a man who had His very nature and character within him. And He wanted me trust Him enough to bring that special man to me in His perfect time. Guess what? In His perfect time, that's exactly what He did. Eric is my gorgeous and gallant knight in shining armor. I am *so* glad I didn't settle for second best.

Too many women become desperate. They are hungry for attention and affection, so they settle for guys who don't know the first thing about how to treat a woman. They are impatient—they don't trust that God could have something better for them. So they compromise. They give themselves to men who really aren't even worth a second glance.

Christlike men who have learned to treat women with dignity and respect are indeed rare. Even guys who hang out at church and wear WWJD wristbands ("What would Jesus do?") often fall short of Christ's standards. Too many Christian men have patterned their actions toward the female sex after one of the many woman-conquering celebrities in Hollywood, rather than after the example of Jesus Christ. But if a woman is aspiring to become a princess of purity, she must wait patiently for a Christlike knight. And though this kind of man is rare, God *is* raising up men after His own heart. And those kinds of men are worth waiting for!

The following true love story portrays a godly woman who knew exactly what kind of man she was waiting for—and she wasn't willing to give her heart away until she was sure she had found him!

A True Test of Love

Lt. John Blanchard was in New York City at Grand Central Station, and he looked up at the big clock. It said five till six.

His heart was racing. At exactly six o'clock he was going to meet the girl whom he thought he was in love with, but had never met. This is what had happened...He had been in Florida for pilot training during World War II, and while he was there he happened to go to a library and check out a book. As he flipped through the pages, he noticed that someone had made notes in the margins. Reading the insightful observations in beautiful handwriting, he said to himself, "I would love to meet whoever wrote these notes—they seem so kind, gentle, and wise."

He looked in the front of the book and saw a name, Harlyss Maynell, New York City. He decided to try to find her. With the help of a New York City phone book, he found her address and wrote her a letter. The day after he wrote her, he was shipped back overseas to fight in the war.

Surprisingly, Harlyss answered John's letter. They soon began to correspond back and forth throughout the war. "Her letters were just like the marvelous notes she had written in that book," John recalled. "She was so comforting and so helping."

One time John had confessed in a letter that he had been scared to death when they flew over Germany. Harlyss had encouraged him, "All brave men are afraid at times. Next time you are afraid, just say 'Yea, though I walk through the valley of the shadow of death, I will fear no evil, for Thou art with me.'"

As they continued to write, John began to realize that he was having romantic feelings toward Harlyss. He wrote, "Send me a picture," and she replied, "No, I won't. Relationships are *not* built on what people look like."

Still, he was intrigued by her and longed to meet her in person. Finally the day came when he was to return to the States on leave. He mentioned in one of his letters that he was coming home and would like to take her to dinner. She had arranged to meet him in New York City's Grand Central

Station at six P.M. under the big clock. "You'll know who I am because I'll be wearing a red rose," she told him.

At last the day had come. John waited nervously to finally meet the girl he thought he loved. Here is how John described his first meeting with Harlyss Maynell:

"A young woman was coming toward me, her figure long and slim. She had blonde hair that lay back in curls from her delicate ears. Her eyes were as blue as flowers. Her lips and chin had a gentle firmness, and in a pale green suit she looked like spring-time come alive!

Excitedly, I started toward her, entirely forgetting to notice that she was *not* wearing a red rose. As I moved her way, she noticed me. A small provocative smile curled her lips.

"Going my way, soldier?" she asked coyly. I took another step closer to her. It was then that I saw...*Harlyss Maynell* with the red rose in her coat, walking directly behind the girl in green. My heart sank. She was a woman well past forty. She was plump. She had graying hair tucked under a worn hat. Her thick ankles were thrust into low shoes. The girl in the green suit was walking quickly away. I had to make a choice. Should I follow after the beauty who had just spoken to me? Or stay and face poor Harlyss Maynell?

I made my decision and I did not hesitate. Turning toward the woman, I smiled. Even as I began to speak, I felt choked by bitter disappointment. "You must be Miss Maynell," I said, extending my hand. "I'm so glad you could meet me. Will you join me for dinner?"

The older woman's face then broadened into a smile. "I don't know what this is all about, son," she replied, "but you know that young woman in the green suit who just went by? I met her on the train. She begged me to wear this rose in my coat. She said that if you should ask me to dinner, to tell you she's waiting for you in that big restaurant across the street. She said it was some kind of a test."[1]

Going for the Gold

The amazing and *romantic* story of John Blanchard and Harlyss Maynell is an incredible example of a young woman who was willing to wait for a man with true integrity—and a man who was rewarded because he did not follow his fleshly desires, but responded with the character of Christ.

The moral of the story is this: Girls, if you will learn to wait patiently and confidently for God to bring a Christlike man into your life, you will not be disappointed. And guys, learn to treat women like the Perfect Gentleman, Jesus Christ. If you do, you will not only be promoted *out* of "jerk-hood," but you will then be worthy of a beautiful princess of purity who is saving herself just for you.

I might add here that this principle of most-guys-are-jerks also has a reverse side. Most girls in today's world are anything *but* a princess of purity. When Eric was in college, he often felt like there were no girls left on the planet who were saving themselves physically, let alone emotionally, for their future husbands. The only exception was his older sister, Krissy. He had to believe that if God had someone like Krissy set aside for a man, then somewhere else in the world God was also molding another woman with that same kind of purity for him.

Women can all too often become manipulative, flirtatious, and self-focused when relating to men. They can play games with a man's heart. They use their priceless pearl of purity for temporary pleasure. While it may be hard for godly women to believe that a Christlike knight exists, it's often equally as difficult for a man of integrity to trust God for a Christlike princess of purity.

To experience a God-written love story, our standards for what we are seeking in a relationship *cannot* be determined by our culture. Our standards should be *radically higher* than the rest of the world. Not that we are going to be perfect or have a perfect relationship, but we should be aiming our arrow at the right target—*applying the very nature and character of Jesus Christ in our attitude toward the opposite sex.*

Many Christians simply don't feel this is a possibility. Their standards sink dangerously low. God's heart must break when He knows the beautiful things He had planned that we often miss because of our foolishness.

I recently read of a youth pastor who counseled a distraught young woman about a relationship she was in. This young girl was head over heels in love with a certain young man. They had been dating a few weeks, and the young man had started pressuring her to have sex with him—and compromise her standards.

"What should I do?" she asked the youth pastor. "I like him so much; I don't want to lose him."

The youth pastor's advice shocked me. He told her to simply be firm with the young man and tell him that if the relationship was going to continue, she could not be pressured to compromise her standards in the area of purity.

"It took a while for the message to sink in to the young man's head," the youth pastor proudly recalled, "but finally he realized where she stood and he respected her. They were able to enjoy a normal healthy dating relationship without her being pressured to give away her virginity."

If that young woman had come to me seeking *my* advice, my response would have been just a little different…"Honey, dump that sleaze-ball so fast he doesn't know what hit him. God has someone better for you than that jerk!" (Okay, so maybe I don't have much patience for guys like that.)

Our goal as followers of Christ should be to pattern our own inward character after His example in how we relate to the opposite sex, and to wait for someone who is governed by His very nature and character in how *they* relate to *us*.

Such a goal may seem unrealistic in today's world. Actually, it *is* unrealistic without leaning upon the Author of true romance. But with His help, let's reach for something *better* than what our culture offers. While our society boasts of a warped and twisted perspective on true love, let's trust Him enough to sing a "sweeter song."

> *God laughs at odds. No matter how big the dream, how huge the request, how lofty the hope, or even how statistically impossible the task, He can do it—and infinitel,y immeasurably more. May God be seen for how great He really is!*
>
> Ephesians 3:20 (paraphrase)

> *If our hopes are being disappointed just now, it means that they are being purified. There is nothing noble the human mind has ever hoped for or dreamed of that will not be fulfilled. One of the greatest strains in life is the strain of waiting for God.*
>
> *"Because thou hast kept the word of my patience."*
>
> *Remain spiritually tenacious.*[2]
>
> Oswald Chambers

A Step Further

Every once in a while it's good to remind ourselves as Christians what we are truly living for. It's good to remind ourselves that we're holding out for something far greater than this world can comprehend. And it's good to reflect upon what that *something* is! Turn the pages of your Bible to the very last book. It's a book called Revelation. Flip to chapter 21 and read to the very end of your Bible. When you read this short portion of God's Word, you will discover a little picture of heaven that you will never forget.

Section Four

Sweetening A Love Story

Chapter Twelve

Eric:

Home Sweet Home

The ultimate test of true love

When I was twelve you were *pretty* cool if you could say the word "dude" five times in one sentence. You were *really* cool if your shoes stunk because you never wore socks. And you were *like totally* cool if you had a pair of corduroy OP shorts.

When I was twelve, shorts were really *short*. Corduroy OPs hugged your rear-end like Saran Wrap around a grapefruit, and seemed to hang maybe a fraction of an inch longer than a pair of Speedos. When these were in, they were *really* in. But when they went out of style, you wouldn't want to be caught dead in a pair of corduroy OPs!

When I was thirteen I had already donated my beloved tan OPs to the Goodwill and was learning to do the moon-walk in parachute pants. It was right at that time, in the height of my pubertized years, that my dad walked into a bargain basement and picked himself out a really cheap pair of totally outdated fluorescent blue corduroy OPs.

"So, what do ya think?" he said to me, as he proudly modeled his "great discovery" in the middle of the living room while the blinds were up.

"Where did you get those?!" I howled in horror, while closing the blinds to make sure the neighbors couldn't see this detestable fashion show.

"I got these babies for three bucks!" he proclaimed while doing a spin in front of the mirror and checking out his tightly packaged rear-end.

"Dad legs" are a sight I believe every young person needs to behold at least once in their lifetime. If not for academic reasons, then just for a little peek into the way things are outside of Hollywood. But I'll warn you—wear your sunglasses! "Dad legs" see the light of the sun approximately once every ten years.

So there was my dad in the middle of our living room. The light was off but you would have never noticed, because my dad's fluorescent blue shorts accompanied by his glowing white "dad legs" were providing plenty of light.

Have you ever noticed that dad's have *no* clue how to wear their socks either? At thirteen, I had started wearing socks again, but they were *always* scrunched down at the ankles. Dads, for some reason, never learn that socks are made to be scrunched. My dad was not only tightly snuggled inside the most outdated and despicable pair of fluorescent blue shorts, with his "dad legs" glowing like the sun coming out of ten years captivity, but he had his socks yanked up to his knee caps. And just when you thought it couldn't get any worse...they were *black dress socks!*

A few weeks passed before I saw "the outfit from Dorksville" again. But this time it wasn't in the safe confines of the Ludy living room. He unveiled it right smack in the middle of our family vacation, before the eyes of untold masses when the Ludy family went out to build a sandcastle on the beach.

"Well, wouldn't this make for a great picture!" My mom excitedly rang with her trusty Polaroid in hand. "Okay now, let's all gather around." Then came the discovery. "Hey! Where's Eric?"

My dad was not only adorned in "the outfit from Dorksville," but he had added a white v-neck undershirt to his prized ensemble. I was a good three hundred yards away, pretending to shop for a metal detector. In fact, it would have taken a high-powered set of binoculars to see me. And if someone had come up to me and said, "Hey! Isn't that your dad over yonder?" I would have denied him three times before the cock crowed!

Disowning our family members is not something we need to be taught how to do. It's something we just somehow become really good at. When my brother, Marky, was fifteen, he worked at Dairy Queen and wore polyester brown pants. He used to have my mom drop him off a quarter mile from work and tell her,

"Okay! Now here's the plan. I'll call you when I'm done and I'll meet you right here. Make sure you don't come *there!*"

He would then proceed to hike to Dairy Queen and always make it look as if he was getting out of a really nice car in the parking lot. Then he would confidently stroll to the door of the restaurant, spinning a set of borrowed keys in his hand and whistling.

We are trained by our culture to be embarrassed about our family. We are educated by our peers in the art of ignoring our parent's advice and belittling them with our words. In fact, we were taught as teenagers that we must attempt to convince the world around us that we are lone-rangers without a family, self-sufficient, and attending school purely for social reasons.

Many of us, over the years, have become professionals at living our lives without family. And most of us have very good reasons, too. Reasons that go beyond our dad's glowing white legs. Reasons that touch us where we hurt and where we feel. If you want to touch a deep nerve in the heart of our generation, all you need to do is bring up the subject of family. Probably over ninety percent of the pain and hurt in a majority of our lives stems directly back to our home-life growing up.

"Eric, what in the world does this have to do with my love life?" you say with a furrowed brow.

That's a fair question. I mean, if talking about family is such a deep issue and causes so much pain and it isn't necessary, then lets skip the heart-rending experience and move on to a little more romance. Well, for those of you who are not inclined to touch this topic, I'm afraid it *is* a necessary issue to include in this book…and a very key harmony line to the "sweeter song."

For many of you, family doesn't seem to fit into your grid of the "beautiful side of love." In fact, it fits better into the "beautiful side of Alzheimer's," when you are finally able to forget all that went wrong in your life.

Well, leaving out family when it comes to your love life is like baking bread without yeast—it will come out flat in the end. Now it's important to understand that family to each and every one of us is different. For some of us it means two parents, a brother, a sister, and a shaggy dog named Waldo. For others it means just a dad or maybe just a mom. There are some whose family consists of simply those few special people who care about them at church.

God designed us to have a family around us. Even if those who have a biological link to us are not near and familiar, He still provides us with special people in our life who can fill in as Dad, Mom, big brother, little sister, and a shaggy dog named Waldo.

So no matter if you have a big family or a little family consisting of fill-ins from the little Baptist Church down the street, this section, if taken to heart, will not only sweeten your love story, but it could very well change your life.

Them

There are four people on the planet earth that can irritate me quicker than any others. I have tremendous patience, boundless grace, and bottomless mercy for seemingly everyone but *these four people.*

I really do desire to be an example of Jesus to *everyone* I meet. I want people to walk away after spending time with me thinking, "That must be what Jesus acts like." There are moments when I really think I'm getting there, then...I get around one of *them.*

Each of us has our "them." Maybe you don't have four; maybe you have two, or maybe you have twenty. But we all have *them.* A good formula for finding the "them" in your life is to look for all of those who share the same last name with you, always get a slice of your birthday cake, and have an exact replica of your nose stuck on their funny looking face. "Them," in your life just as in mine, are familiar. Awfully familiar! You know everything from the bad jokes they always try to crack to their personal body fragrance.

Really the only requirement for a "them" in our lives is *familiarity.* Or, if "familiarity" is too vague a word, how about this one...*family.* Yes, it's true! Everyone else in the world may be bamboozled into thinking that we are perfect angels, but our family will *always* know the truth.

If you were to take a peek inside the windows of my home while I was growing up, you would have wonderful blackmail material on me now. I was a "Christian," but strangely, you wouldn't have ever confused me with St. Francis of Assisi. I was anything but Christlike as I roamed the hallways of my home.

In a matter of three seconds I could scream, "What are you doing? This is my room you big Stink! Get outa here! Hey! Turn it back! I was watching the game! Meatloaf for dinner? I hate meatloaf!" We for some reason feel very comfortable venting all of our pent-up frustrations on those who make the mistake of being related to us.

We demand that our family be perfect, and we don't allow room for error. Let me make a case in point. If one of you accidentally stepped on my big toe—and I mean you really smooshed it—my response to *you* as compared to the way I would respond to *my brother*, if he did it, is *strangely* different.

To you I would gasp, "That's all right!" And even if my face was fire-red and my cheeks were bloated from containing my yelp, I would say, "Those things happen! I'll survive!"

You see, to *you* I would offer grace. I would excuse your mistake. Now my brother on the other hand...he should know better than to smoosh the big toe of his older brother. My response to him would be a little more animated.

"Hey!" I would scream. "What do you think you're doing? Watch where you're walking!" Then, as is appropriate for all good and healthy brotherly encounters, I would give him a hard shove.

It's difficult for us to extend grace to the "them" in our lives. We often expect *them* to live at a higher standard of perfection than anyone else on the planet.

But it doesn't stop here. Not only do those closest to us get under our skin and irritate us, but they can also wound us in a way no one else can.

If you came up to me and said, "Eric you stink, you're ugly, and I hate you!" I would probably step back, blink a couple of times, and then say, "Well, ah, thanks for being so blunt!" I would go home and tell Leslie about what you said and probably even feel rejected as I recalled the episode. Then Leslie would tenderly wrap her arm around my should and say, "Eric, that's ridiculous! They are probably on drugs or something!"

Your words might sting for a little while and might cause me to put on an extra puddle of cologne before I head out into public, but I *would* get over your words. Why? Because, *you're not my family!*

If my *dad* came up to me and said, "Eric, you stink, you're ugly, and I hate you!" I would be absolutely devastated. Any number of comforting words from Leslie wouldn't be able to bandage up the wound that my dad's words would make in my heart and mind. *Your* words would hurt, but *my dad's* words would cripple. Because, *you* would be just an opinion; *my dad* is my "definition of reality."

Our generation is lying crippled on the side of life's road because of the words of those most "familiar" with us. There are many of you reading this book who think of yourself as "stupid," because those who knew you best when growing up always said you were "stupid." Many of you are convinced that you are "fat." Why? Because your family always told you that you were "fat." Then there are those of you who, in your mind, are "ugly" simply because the word "ugly" has been used by your little brother to describe your face since you were in kindergarten. It is family who defines our reality. Even if they are lying, we can't help but believe family— because if anyone should know...it's *them!*

It's no wonder that many of us abandon the family ship as soon as we get the chance. We want to escape the irritants, the bosses, the nitpickers, the know-it-alls. We head out into this great big world in search of a *different* family. You see, we all desire to belong. God designed us for companionship and for teammates. We just don't do well alone. Some of us try to find it in friends, some of us look for it in sports, and some of us even attempt to find it in our shaggy dog named Waldo. But when we run from the "them" and try and patch up our need with "our choice" of fill-ins, *instead of God's choice,* we will never cover the ache. We *need* family! We need our "them!" And *not* just as the solution to loneliness, but as the secret ingredient to successful romance.

When we condition ourselves to run away and disown those who are most familiar with us, we're preparing ourselves for a disastrous future. Our lives consist of relationships. God designed us for family. Intimate family relationships are one of the most difficult things we must deal with as humans, because closeness leads to the exposure of who we *really* are, inside and outside. We young people have a very short period in our life that God seems to give us for practice. The Denver Broncos have a pre-season in which they hone their football skills, study the plays, and scrimmage. In the same way, we all have our pre-marriage season in which we need to hone our family skills, study the relationship's play book, and to learn how to be like Christ to the "them" in our life.

Family isn't just in our past; it's very much in our future, too. And I guarantee you, that if you train yourself to model Christ *now* to those most familiar and close, you will be superb at it when you get married.

Our Practice Field

When I was nineteen God got ahold of my life. All the excitement I had for the Denver Broncos went directly into my love relationship with Jesus Christ. Everywhere I went I would tell people about Jesus, and everyone who knew me before "the change" thought I had just taken a dip in the loony pond. I was a new Eric! I was loving people, serving people, and even hugging people. I was a great big bundle of angelic compassion everywhere I went, except when it came time for me to go…home. I was a changed man, throwing a great big love party! The problem was my family never received the invitation.

I'll never forget the day the tall lanky stranger muttered the words. I have heard many words in my life. Most of them have traveled down my ear canal at the speed of light, never even slowing down for as much as an hors d'oeuvre before exiting out the other side. But these words stuck. They sat their gigantic derrière down, made themselves comfortable in my cranium, and let it be known that they were there to stay.

"Did you know that you are only as holy," the skinny man said, "as you are in your home?"

I was a good Christian. I had given Jesus Christ my entire ship. I was learning to love, to guard the treasure of my purity, and to be faithful to my future spouse. I didn't know anyone else who was doing *that!* But God was showing me,

Eric, if you're not able to act like Jesus now with those most close and familiar, then what makes you think when you get married that you are going to be an example of Jesus to your wife? Eric, you are only as Christlike as you are Christlike around your family. If you start there, where it is most difficult to love, then it will be easy to display Christ everywhere else!

Family is our practice field. We take into our future marriage what we learn in our life with "them" in the here and now. If we learn to snub and disown those closest to us now, we're setting habit patterns for broken trust and emotional heartache in the future. If we train ourselves in the here and now to verbally abuse our family members, we will be conditioning ourselves to bite rather than bless in the future.

When I was eight, my mom signed me up for piano lessons. I loved to tinker but I hated the practice. Practice is the most grueling aspect of success. But when the day of the recital came, I was always very glad my mom had forced me to practice. Because I was prepared, I was a whole lot less likely to make a fool of myself in front of the crowd.

A Step Further

The next time you feel like running away from home and changing your name, read the story of Joseph in the book of Genesis, chapters 37 through 47. If you thought you had it bad, just wait till you get a glimpse of *his* sibling rivalry.

Chapter Thirteen

Eric:
Training to Be Tender

*How your own personal
oddballs can prepare you for romance*

Learn to Forgive and Be Forgivable

*As a proper thank-you to God for selecting you
for this new life of love, put on the clothes that
He purchased for you and so generously placed in
your spiritual closet: compassion, kindness, humility,
silent confidence, and patience. Not haughty, hurtful,
and holding grudges; but humble, helpful, and happy
to forgive those who have wronged you just as thoroughly as Jesus forgave you. But more important
than any other piece of clothing in your entire
wardrobe, put on love. It's the key to the entire outfit,
bringing out the sparkle in all the other elements.*

Colossians 3:12-14 (paraphrase)

Marriage is a lifestyle chucked full of asking forgiveness and offering forgiveness. It doesn't seem to matter how hard I try to emulate Jesus, my sin nature finds its way to the surface of my life. As I mentioned earlier, Leslie calls my belligerent and cranky nature my "poopy side." There are days that I must ask Leslie over one hundred times to forgive me. If there were an Olympic event for offering mercy and forgiveness, I believe she could easily win the gold.

Each of us should train for such an Olympic event. Learning to forgive takes hard work and many tears. It takes determination and a whole lot of help from God.

It might seem nearly impossible to forgive your family for some of the things they did to you while you were growing up. But if you make it your goal to forgive them as God has forgiven you, and if you actively pursue loving them the way Christ loves you, then you will not only have set your own heart free, but you will have showcased a little picture of heaven on earth. If you learn to forgive, you will have learned the greatest defense mechanism against divorce.

Forgiving is hard. But often times, it is even more difficult to be *forgivable*. Most of us complain about how we have been wronged by our families, but we fail to realize that we ourselves have been guilty of hurting them, too. Let me show you a little video clip from my life.

Marky

Growing up as an older brother, I had a sacred duty—to make sure my younger brother, Marky, realized that he was nothing but a dirtball. Older brotherhood is an art. I learned how to be a tough older brother by watching Tim Miller. He was the gargantuan big brother of my good friends Danny and Darren.

He had a wounded-mule-strut, and as he walked he would snarl and move his mouth around as if he were chewing on a huge wad of gum. When he came strolling through the living room one day, I remember blurting out with my high squeaky twelve-year-old voice, "Hey, Tim!"

His response was legendary. He boomed, "Hey!" in the deepest, most bassy voice I had ever heard. Then he did a little head nod with his eyes all squinty and strutted out of the room.

From that day on, whenever I spoke to Marky, it was with my best rendition of a bassy voice blended perfectly with the head nod and the squinty eye.

Big brotherhood is easy for some. But not for me! I just had to get stuck with a little brother who is two-and-a-half years younger than me, but looked older than me. All of our years growing up, Marky was a half-inch shorter than me but he weighed *more* than me. He, of course, was built like a football linebacker. And as my mom exhorted me, "Well, Eric, you're built more like a golfer!"

Well, I didn't want to be a golfer! I wanted to be a football player! God had somehow messed up and given Marky the brawn he was supposed to have given me. Since I was certain my scrawniness was a direct result of Marky's being in my life, I was determined to make him pay.

For twenty years I never once spoke a compliment to my little brother. In fact as the years passed, I became more cruel and more heartless. Don't get me wrong, I loved him; I just would never allow *him* to discover that. He was my emotional punching bag, my stress reliever. I stuffed my anger all day long and then vented it on him.

There was also a brotherly pride that acted like steel armor around my heart. I could never lose at anything to him, I could never show any tender emotion in front of him, and *never* would you catch me with my arms wrapped around him in hug formation.

A Ludy Christmas morning has many traditions. I absolutely love *almost all* of them. But there is one that seriously violated my older brother comfort zone growing up. It's the one that states, "Whenever a Ludy receives a gift from a person in the family, that Ludy must stand up, walk across the room, and with a great big smile of gratitude shimmering on their face, give that generous family member...*a hug!*"

No way! There was *no* possible way I was going to drape my older brother arms around my stinkin' little brother's body. It inevitably happened that either he opened up his gift from me, or else I unwrapped my gift from him. All Ludys around the Christmas tree leaned in with wonder scribbled across their faces. Marky and I awkwardly arose from our chairs and fumbled to the center of the room, both of us staring at the carpet. Ludy tradition stated that I had to give him a hug. But "signs of affection" are clearly delineated in the "Big Brother's Bible" as "gross and deeply disturbing." So we invented our own version of a Christmas thank-you. We called it "The Bump."

With my deep bassy voice, my snarl, and my squinty eye, I droned, "Thanks." Then we clanked elbows and both strutted like the wounded mule back to our seats.

All my growing up years I referenced the wrong "bible" to figure out successful behavior in relationships. Here I was at the age of twenty, still strutting around, still booming with my bassy voice, and still criticizing those closest and most dear to me. Before I was ready for a family of my own, I had to learn to bring my example of Jesus into my own home.

Discovering a Best Friend

It was just a normal night in March. I had no idea it was a night of destiny. The shutters didn't shake and the lights didn't flicker. I was totally caught off guard!

I was home from college, my grandparents were visiting, and I was booted out of *my* room and stuck in my *brother's* room, next to his bed on a cot. I probably came into Marky's hangout and threw my stuff on the cot and boomed with my tough raspy voice, "I'm sleeping in here!"

I was the same old Eric when I entered his room that night, but when I left in the morning, I was a new man. I remember trying to get comfortable on the stone-like mattress and staring up at the light on the ceiling. My night of destiny began to unfold midway through my nightly conversation with God.

"Jesus, make me like You!" I remember boldly stating, "Whatever it takes, make me like You!" It wasn't but a millisecond later that God responded. I often jokingly warn people to be careful about what they pray. Even if you don't take what you pray seriously, God sure does! In fact, if you want to know God exists, pray that prayer. He just loves to respond to it!

In that moment, with my eyes transfixed upon the ceiling light, I knew, beyond a shadow of a doubt, what God wanted me to do. I call it the "blowfish feeling." I knew precisely what I needed to do, but there was just no possible way I could ever do it. I felt like my body was expanding and I was going to blow-up! My palms were moist and my heart was banging around inside my rib cage like a toddler with a kitchen pot.

If you are an older sibling, you will totally relate. As an older brother, I had become a master at making my younger brother feel worthless. Now, after an entire lifetime of criticism and cruelty, how was I supposed to...*ask his forgiveness?* Ten thousand tender and tear-filled hugs with my brother sounded better than *that!*

"God, I can't!" I mournfully remonstrated with a ghost-like countenance. "I know I just prayed that prayer, but there is just no way I can do *that!*"

As I anxiously rustled on the stone-like cot that fateful night, feeling like a blowfish about to blow, I had to make a choice. A choice between relational stupidity and relational success. But, even more directly, it was a choice between my big ego and my little brother.

My deep voice, which was usually lower than a snake's belly, squeaked like a parakeet going through puberty, as I said, "Marky?" All my older brother toughness came flopping to the ground with one gigantic thud, as my little brother responded with *his* tough bassy drone, "Yeah?"

"Marky?" I again haltingly sputtered, "Uh...I don't quite know how to say this, but...I...I'm sorry!" Silence filled the room and tears filled my eyes. My brother hadn't seen tears in my eyes since the time I electrocuted myself when I was four. Now here I was, swallowing hard, with my lip quivering, *right in front of him!*

"I've been a horrible brother!" I confessed. "I have never once complimented you. I have only torn you down. I've spent my life telling you what you do wrong, but I've never told you about all that you do right. I have built up so much pride between us, Marky!"

With tears flowing down my cheeks, I said, "Please forgive me! I *really* want to be your friend and not just your brother!"

I was Marky's hero! He had dreamed of this moment. With all the things I had done to him, he could have very easily laughed and left the room. I wouldn't have blamed him. But I'll never forget Marky's wet eyes looking into mine. His words were full of sincerity and love. "I forgive you."

We prayed together as a twosome for the very first time. If ever in my life I have been convinced God was smiling, it was during that prayer. I'm certain all heaven was listening.

When we concluded our first prayer as true brothers, I knew there was one more thing God wanted me to do.

"God, you are really pushing it!" I groaned.

I looked up at Marky and whispered, "Uh, there's something else I think we, ah, (gulp) need to do."

All Marky said was, "I know."

We both got up from our beds, opened our arms wide, and *hugged* for the very first time!

I have often said that I discovered my best friend that plain, ordinary night in March of 1991. But what I also discovered was the beautiful truth of how to have a successful relationship with those closest and most familiar. You have to learn to be *forgivable!*

Probably everyone reading this book can identify with my Marky story in some way, shape, or form. We all have our "them." We all need to realize that God has given the *them* to us for the sake of practice. If you learn to be forgiving and forgivable with those in your life now, you will be great at it with your future family as well.

A wise older man once told me, "Humility, Eric, is measured by how quickly you can admit that you are wrong."

Well, by that definition, I was one proud dude when I was growing up! But it was never too late for me to discover success in relating to those closest to me. If we make a conscious decision today to seek humility, God can turn all our past haughtiness into evidences of His wondrous grace in our lives.

> *Do no pray for easy lives! Pray to be stronger men.*
> *Do not pray for tasks equal to your powers.*
> *Pray for powers equal to your tasks.*
> *Then the doing of your work shall be no miracle, but you shall be a miracle.*[1]
>
> Phillip Brooks

Learn to Cherish "Them"

Yes, family can be embarrassing at times! My dad had his fluorescent blue shorts, and my mom sang the "Hallelujah Chorus" in the grocery store checkout line (that was one of her many creative and loud ways to be a Christian witness). My sister was voted "most quiet" by her classmates, and Marky was...well, Marky!

Those closest to us often seem like oddballs. It always seems like everyone else on the planet is normal, but our family is from outer space.

"My dad has hair growing out of his ears, and he thinks it makes him look distinguished!" blurted an anonymous contributor with a chuckle. "My mom takes her gum out at dinner time and sticks it behind her ear for later!" howled another contributor who desires to remain nameless. The truth is, we as humans, *all* have idiosyncrasies. We all have our own version of hair-ridden ears with gum stuck behind them.

When you get married you'll understand that even *your spouse* has oddball characteristics. I mean, just imagine what Leslie thought the first time she saw me having a serious business conversation at five in the morning with nothing on but my stylish Fruit-of-the-Looms. To Leslie that was outrageous; to me that was business as usual.

Learning to loyally stand by those who embarrass us is a character trait of Christ. Just think! Where would you be with God right now if He didn't hang around those of us who embarrass Him? Loyalty is also a necessary quality in a successful marriage relationship.

Leslie's parents told me before I married her, "Eric, the little quirks that you and Leslie both have can either be a source of irritation in your relationship or a source of humor and enjoyment. You need to learn how to cherish the funny little things both of you do!"

I like that word "cherish." If we learn how to find intimate pleasure in the unique way God has crafted those closest to us, we could turn what usually causes us to run away, into an opportunity for great enjoyment and fun.

My family has learned to laugh at all of our oddball characteristics. When we get together, we just howl about my dad's OPs. We roll on the floor when we realize that now all the Ludy kids are the ones singing the "Hallelujah Chorus" in the checkout line. And tears come to our eyes because we're laughing so hard, when we talk about all that poor Leslie has to put up with in being married to a Ludy.

We each have a choice. We can either brand our families as embarrassing, or we can learn to take delight in their craziness. We can either run from them to save our precious reputations, or we can learn to be like Christ and cherish both their nerdy side right along with their nice, neat, and noble side. Because, *that* is what marriage is all about. Just ask Leslie!

Learn to Serve "Them"

Let me remind you once again. The way you behave around those most intimate and familiar to you is precisely the way you will behave around your future spouse someday.

I'll never forget my mom, with her hands on her hips and a scowl on her face, pounding this point home to her disagreeable fourteen-year-old son…"Eric, the way you treat *me* is the way you are going to treat your *wife!*"

My response was anything but remorseful and sweet. I countered, "I'm gonna treat her better than *that!*"

You see, I was convinced that when my wife came into my life, my knight in shining armor side would finally appear and I would treat her like a princess. I mean, I loved my mom and all, but *not* like *that!* When my radiant lover came into my life, I would be mesmerized with her beauty. I was certain that married life would tap into my sweeter more sensitive side. Unfortunately for both you and me, that is just not true.

Don't get me wrong! It *is* true that your spouse will hold a place in your heart, mind, and life that your mom or dad could never fill. And it *is* true that it will be easier at first to put your most sensitive foot forward. But it is *also* true that the closer and more familiar you get with your spouse, the more your true self seeps out. And the person you have spent your life training to be, will become unveiled. For most of us, that is *not* a good thing!

Leslie has thanked God a myriad of times that I had a season in my life when God taught me how to treat my mom and sister with sensitivity. For three years, from the age of twenty to the age of twenty-three, I made it one of my primary focuses in life to practice being a true gentleman. It wasn't easy! Not because of *them* but because of *me!* I had gotten so use to spouting off whatever thoughts came into my mind. I had to learn that women take words a little more seriously then men. Statements such as, "Are you really going to wear that dress?" and "Boy, you look totally exhausted!" and "Whoever cooked this stroganoff needs to learn how to use an oven!" and "Are you pregnant or just preparing for winter?" were now completely *off-limits!*

It was in this three year period that I learned to get up after dinner, and without even being asked, immediately wash the dishes. Now, guys, don't ask me why, but that dish washing thing has a powerful effect on women! I learned, though I was scared to death to do it, to simply say, "Is there any way that I can help?"

There are two ways that each of us can approach life. Spending our days meeting *our* needs, or looking for ways to meet *other's* needs. The mystery is that when we spend our life focused on our own needs, we are never satisfied, and our deepest needs never seem to be met. But when we pour out our life and focus on how we can serve others, we find not only incredible fulfillment, but our deepest needs are met as well! Learning to serve leads to the "happily ever after" finish you've always dreamed of.

What am I to do? I expect to pass through this world but once. Any good work, therefore, any kindness, or any service I can render to any soul of man...let me do it now. Let me not neglect or defer it, for I shall not pass this way again.[2]

An old Quaker saying

Be careful not to allow any words that are dirty, disrespectful, or damaging slip from your lips. Use

*your words to build, not burden; to help, not harm;
and to encourage, not exasperate.*

Ephesians 4:29 (paraphrase)

The Secret to Winning a Heart

I'm convinced, after studying the female species for twenty-eight years, that girls wear perfume *not* to impress us guys, but to impress other girls! Just think about it. If a girl really wanted to dowse herself in a fragrance that would magnetically pull a guy to her side, she would pour on something that smelled like a spicy chicken burrito!

The same is true with us guys. We lift weights, grunt, sweat, pull hamstrings, twist ankles, and stink, all to impress the girls. When in actuality, it's only really the guys who are impressed. When we guys see an enormous Arnold Schwarzenegger look-alike, we gasp, "Wow! He's huge!" Most of the girls only notice the fact that his neon pink spandex don't match his obnoxious forest green and apple red muscleshirt, which smells strangely akin to a skunk that died a couple of weeks ago.

Part of what makes marriage both fun and exciting is learning to appreciate the little things your spouse works so hard at. Leslie has very little appreciation for an enormous muscle. Which is really a good thing, because if she did, she wouldn't have married me! I'm one of those builds that my mom calls "wiry." I have absolutely no excess *anything* on my body. I don't have a spare tire around the middle, but I also don't have a whole lot of spare muscle hanging out on my body either. If I stop lifting weights for just one week, I shrivel up like a raisin on a hunger strike, and I'm at risk of the next big gust of wind carrying me away. So I work hard at keeping weight on, especially muscle. And Leslie, the student of Eric Ludy that she is, has learned how important it is that she notices my muscles, even if they are miniscule.

I arrive home from the gym and there's my Love waiting for me. With a great big smile and eyes awide with excitement she says, "Let me see 'em!" At that I scrunch up my sleeve and flex my mammoth biceps (at least she acts like it is). "Wow!" she proclaims as she squishes it. Girls, it might not make any sense to you, but when you act impressed over something that a man works hard at, even something as small as one of my muscles, it makes him feel like a champion.

The same thing happens in reverse when I crawl into Leslie's world and learn to appreciate the little things that she works hard at. Leslie is a great shopper! I am not! I am very good at *saving* money, *not* spending it. Leslie is very good at what she calls, "saving money while she spends it." A very subtle difference, but one that has ruined more than a few marriages. As weird as this might sound, I have learned to have fun shopping with Leslie. I have made it a point to spend time in her world and attempt to enjoy myself. Leslie would note that my "poopy" side can still surface during such shopping ventures, but all in all we have learned to have a great time together searching for just the right sweater for those pants, and the appropriate belt to go with that shirt.

When we get married we inevitably discover that we are very different from the one to whom we just said, "I do." We cover up a lot of those differences when we are falling in love, but marriage is total nakedness. Who we are behind all our fine apparel is seen in all its glory when we move in together. Leslie use to think my breath always smelled like wintergreen Binaca. When she woke up next to me one newly wedded morning and caught a whiff of the "breath of death," she found out how wrong she was!

Shut Up and Snuggle

Leslie and I had been married for about three weeks when she began to act sort of funny. There she was sitting on the end of our bed crying. The problem was, she was crying for no reason. As a guy, I cry when I have something to cry about. But Leslie, I discovered, cries just to cry.

I sat down next to her and said, "Les? What's wrong?" You see, as a guy I like to figure out the problem. Why? So I can fix it! "Come on Les! Tell me what happened so I can help!"

What really confused me was that Leslie cried even harder after I offered help. You would think she would want me to help her fix her life. I mean, if *I* were crying that is what *I* would want her to do for me. Right there was my problem! As long as I tried to meet Leslie's needs in the way I desired my needs to be met in *my world,* I only made things worse. The only way I can help Leslie is when I crawl into *her world* and look at meeting her needs through *her* eyes. What I find is shocking!

She wants me to shut up! Strangely, she doesn't even want her problem solved. She just wants me to be there, to validate her feelings, and to wrap my arm around her shoulder and squeeze.

Girls, you might think it is obvious that a guy should just know to do that. But I'm telling you today that it's the farthest thing from our minds! Since we, as guys, usually want our problems solved, we naturally feel that the best way to be sensitive to a girl would be to help her solve her problems, too. Despite the fact that we guys are often bumbling idiots when it comes to sensitivity…don't think we aren't trying!

If you want to win a heart, you need to be tender. Tenderness is the quality of slipping into someone else's world and caring for them in the way "their world" defines as "the best way of meeting my needs."

Guys—being a shoulder to cry on, speaking words that remind a woman of your affection, doing the dishes after dinner, and making sure she has a full tank of gas before she hits the road to go shopping—these are all simple little things that you can do to tenderly care for a woman. Because in her world, those little things are huge!

Girls, if you want a few hints on winning a guy's heart, just talk with Leslie. She is the absolute best at it! You know what she calls me? All you guys are going to be jealous! She clasps her hands together, tilts her head, smiles with wonder, and in her sweet and adorable voice, she calls me her *Hero!* Girls, if you want to grab a guy's heart, then ennoble him with your words. When a man is respected and honored by a woman, he gains thirty-six pounds of sheer muscle instantly, can outrun a bullet train, and can leap a skyscraper in a single bound. Words of respect are what transform mere men into superheroes. So whether it is squeezing his muscles, showing interest in his rock collection, or calling him your hero, a dash of tenderness in the way you treat a man means the difference between being married to a gentle-man or a gingerbread-man. One is heroic and tender; the other is stale and cut out of the same mold as the rest of them.

If you are ever going to win the heart of your lover someday, you need to start practicing tenderness *now*. And just like learning to forgive and be forgivable, and learning to cherish and to serve, your practice ground is none other than your family.

I guarantee you that if you can learn to be sweet and tender with the "them" in your life, your future lover's heart will be like putty in your hands.

Moms and Sisters

Guys, if your mothers and sisters are still in near proximity, they are wonderful training wheels for us as we learn how to navigate this brand new world called "women." The reason I recommend mothers and sisters is not only because they are the most difficult to practice on, but also because they are some of the few women on the planet who won't misinterpret our tenderness as a proposal for marriage. If you don't have a mother or sister, just use extreme discretion on whom you choose to practice. Because tenderness really does work!

Okay, now guys—if tenderness is a foreign concept to you, then putting it into practice will be a bit strange at first. But I promise, the more you do it the more natural it will seem. First, I want you to begin to look for opportunities to compliment these dear women in your life. Whether it is their hair, their stunning outfit for church, their amazing singing voice, or even their incredible sense of humor, learn to notice the little things that are important in their world.

Second, I want you to speak it out loudly and so that *they* can hear it. Tell them how beautiful they look, how nice their voice sounds, or how fun they are to be around. They will undoubtedly be shocked when you first transform into a gentleman, but your consistency will convince them that "Jerksville" is a thing of the past.

Third, learn to be a student of women. You might think that you already are, but most guys don't realize that there is far more to a woman than just her physical beauty. You need to become a student of how a woman works on the *inside*. If you desire a "happily ever after" romance, you will need to learn how to study the inner workings of the female gender.

I remember being nineteen and extremely *un*-tender. My mom was having a "bad hair day." She was teary and frustrated with the color of the kitchen cabinets, she thought the tee shirt I was wearing should be thrown out, and she thought my dad should tell his boss to jump in a frozen lake. Finally, at about three in the afternoon she yelled out, "I just need to get out of this house!"

I was in the kitchen approximately four feet from my mother, clothed in my raggedy tee shirt. I carefully thought through what my mom had just spoken, and then replied, "You just went to the store today!"

Let me warn all young men who are still unmarried. Never, and I mean NEVER respond to a woman the way I just did. You see, when a woman speaks, there is a difference between the precise definition of what she says and the actual meaning behind her words. When a woman says, "I just need to get out of this house!" her meaning goes far beyond walking out onto the front porch and watching neighborhood traffic pass by. I still don't have it figured out, but I think it has more to do with a candlelit dinner out, purchasing a new outfit from Saks Fifth Avenue, and a quick stop by the jewelry store just to browse and drop hints. But it is only *the student* of women who would pick up on that *slight* differentiation.

Finally, learn to just shut-up and be a shoulder to cry on. And *don't solve,* just *snuggle.* When your mom or sister doesn't make sense, don't force her to be rational; rather learn to take your arm and place it around her shoulder and squeeze.

Dads and Brothers

Girls, I must admit that *your* training wheels for learning tenderness are a whole lot more challenging to put on. It is usually fairly easy to be tender to dads...it's *brothers* who pose the bigger problem.

Brothers, like me, tend to be ninety-five percent Jerk, four percent Gross, and one percent Tender. Most sisters would probably say one percent is a little too generous! Basically, we are in desperate need of a little schooling when it comes to learning how treat a lady, let alone how to win her heart.

Sisters, this is where *you* come in. Please have mercy on us "jerky" guys and learn to be tender with us. In fact, if only for the sake of the girls that we will one day marry, help prepare us to be true gentlemen. Look at it as a wedding gift to your future sister-in-law. Whether you realize it or not, a man is shaped by the words of a woman. If they are words that belittle, even the strongest man in the world could be made a wimp. But if they are words that build-up, even the biggest wimp could be transformed into a world-leader.

First, crawl into a guy's world (wear a nose plug) and observe what in our world is important. Every guy is different, so you can't just say food and football. It might be music and muscle-shirts, or maybe computers and cap guns.

Next, find opportunities to discuss these "fascinating" topics with him. If you venture into *his* world, you will discover that he really does have more to him than grunting and sweating. And just as you desire to hear words that make you feel *cherished*, we as guys need words spoken to us that make us feel *respected*.

The next time you see your brother doing something that he excels in, honor him with an exclamation of his prowess, and let him know that you are proud to be his sister. You will find that the more you verbally invest respect, the more a man will understand how to be respectful himself.

And finally, don't try and change us to be more like a girl. Learn to appreciate manhood for all that God created it to be. Maybe it's not naturally as sweet and beautiful as womanhood, but with a little help from the women in our life, we can have a version of sweetness and beauty that is a perfect blend of toughness and tenderness and one hundred percent male.

This might sound like a betrayal to the male species, but there are times when even we guys don't make sense. In those times, we *too* need a shoulder to cry on.

A Sweetened Love Story

Let's get back to the "sweeter song." We all long for the "beautiful side of love" and the "happily ever after" kind of romance. But are we willing to do what it takes to get it? As we discussed earlier in the book, the "sweeter song" is played in the life that empties itself for God, abandons itself to trust Him, and seeks to model Him with every action, attitude, and word. The "sweeter song" is more a *gift* than a *goal*. It's not something we *earn,* it is something we *receive* as we allow the Great Author of romance to masterfully shape us into a gentle and sensitive lover, just like our Bridegroom, Jesus.

Family, as I mentioned earlier, is a piece of our lives that many of us would rather discard. But the "sweeter song" is dependent upon your learning to forgive and be forgivable, to cherish those close and familiar, to serve those who often seem the most difficult to serve, and to tenderly care for the near and dear ones.

If you discard those oddballs in your life called family, you will have thrown away your own private training ground for a divine romance. If you don't learn now to be like Christ in the way you treat "them" in your life, it will be that much more difficult to treat your "them-of-the-future" with the dignity and love they will desperately need.

A Step Further

It isn't a long story, and it is a must read. Genesis chapter 44 and 45 depict one of the most tender scenes of family forgiveness and reconciliation ever. Who in your family do you need to forgive? And to which family members do you need to ask forgiveness? Don't delay! The best time to make things right is *today!*

Chapter Fourteen

Leslie:
Playing for Keeps

*Preparing for success
by picking a winning team*

A Head-On Lesson

As a sixteen-year-old new driver, I was a serious safety hazard to the lovely state of Colorado. Yes, I had taken driver's ed. classes, but I had spent most of those hours writing notes to friends or dozing off, rather than actually learning anything about the important skill of operating a motor vehicle.

When I finally got my license (don't ask me how I passed the driver's test!) I was so excited to have my freedom! I supposedly no longer needed Mom or Dad to accompany me whenever I took the car for a little spin. I was absolutely convinced that I could do it alone.

There were a few minor details that I had failed to learn while snoozing in driver's ed. class. However, I was confident that I would easily figure out anything that I might have missed once I actually got out there and started driving.

One bright January afternoon, I needed to drive across town for an appointment. My parents nervously eyed me as I grabbed the car keys and headed out the door. "Do you want someone to go with you, Leslie?" they questioned.

Impatiently I shook my head. "I don't need *help*," I informed them with a horrified look, as if they had just offered to cut my pancakes into bite-size pieces for me. They looked at each other in genuine concern, but decided to let me go alone anyway. I excitedly bounced out to the car, jumped in, cranked up the radio, and stepped on the gas.

As I pulled up to an intersection and coasted into the left turn lane, all reason left. Was I supposed to go *around* the median? Or turn in front of it? There were no cars coming the other direction to help me see which way to turn, and I began to panic. As the arrow turned green, I brilliantly concluded that I should turn in *front* of the median rather than going around it. At that moment a car came toward me, head-on, and I realized I had just made a not-so-subtle driving mistake! My mind raced. *I don't think they covered this in driver's ed.,* I finally concluded as I pondered what to do. The oncoming traffic that was rapidly collecting angrily honked at me. I shakily pulled backwards out of the wrong lane and went *around* the median, my cheeks burning with humiliation. It was one of my more embarrassing moments, to say the least.

One of the traits we naturally possess as humans is the headstrong determination to do things *our* way, and to do things *alone*. In our culture it is seen as a sign of weakness to actually seek help from someone else. And yet, as Christians, God designed us to *need each other*—He designed us to lean upon the Body of Christ for support, prayer, wisdom, and even practical help. Stubbornly heading off into the wild blue yonder all alone, without assistance from others, often leads us straight into oncoming traffic, and sometimes even causes a head-on collision! This is especially true in the area of our love life.

Choosing a Team

One of the most commonly asked questions from a single person who is longing for a God-written love story is, "How will I know when a relationship is from God?"

To help answer that perplexing question and to prepare for real success in the area of romance—we need to develop a *team*. Our team should be made up of godly people who can keep us accountable to our commitments, pray with us, and provide a refreshing outside perspective on the ups and downs of our journey through life.

Look at the people in *your* life who God may have provided for that very purpose. When you find your teammates and invite them to share in this part of your life, you will discover a sense of beauty and security you never knew was possible.

No longer will you have to "figure things out" on your own—you will be supported by people who love you and will stand beside you. These teammates can provide confirmation and wisdom in helping you discern God's will for your love life.

Why Parents Make Good Teammates

For most of us, the most obvious teammates God has given to us are our *parents*. I know, I know...many of you *were* excited about the idea of teammates, but as soon as you saw the word *parents* you wanted to slam this book shut! Parents seem to often be the *antithesis* of romance! However, I am *not* talking about pre-arranged marriages! And I am not talking about surrendering your love life to your parents. I am simply suggesting you *invite* your parents to be on your team, as you seek God's heart for your love life. You might be surprised what happens when you do, for many reasons...

Parents have an intrinsic, God-given wisdom for our life. When we are young it usually drives us crazy, but as we become mature, this "wisdom" is something that we can learn to cherish. It can be invaluable when we are confused over a relationship. Whether or not we appreciate their "advice," the opinions of our parents should definitely be evaluated seriously before God.

When we honor our parent's God-given position in our life, we honor God. He will bless our decision to honor our parents, even if it isn't easy (Eph.6:1-3).

When I first began to truly learn how to give God the pen to write my love story, one of the first things I felt Him lead me to do was to invite my parents to be on my team through prayer and accountability. It was as if He softly reminded me,

Leslie, I have placed your parents in your life for a reason. They have a special wisdom and anointing that I have given them, especially for your life. Don't ignore the built-in teammates I've provided for you.

Yet the thought of my parents being involved in my *love life* was uncomfortable. After all, I had grown up in a culture that taught me to become "independent" from my parents.

I was a young adult, living a responsible life. Why did I suddenly need my parent's help? Though I was making my own decisions and my parents were treating me as an adult, I still somehow pictured them seeing me as a twelve-year-old in need of strict supervision when it came to this area of my life. In my far-fetched imagination I think I envisioned hesitantly telling them,

"Okay, Mom and Dad, I really want your help in discerning God's will for my love life."

Then I pictured them rubbing their hands together with wicked glee and replying, "Well, it's about time! We already have your husband picked out for you! His name is Alfred Fluffinguffer and the wedding's next month."

That scenario couldn't have been further from reality. My parents were just as concerned with my happiness in this area as I was. And when I came to them and invited them to be "on my team" in helping me seek God about my love life, they responded quite differently than my wild imaginations.

"Leslie, we love you. You and your brothers are more important to us than anything else in the world. We have been praying for your future husband since the day we became Christians. We don't have things all figured out, but we want you to know that we are here for you, any time you need us. We will pray with you whenever you need it, and we will try to provide you with support during these important years of your life."

The freedom and security that came with their words was amazing! The first step had been giving God the pen to write my love story—learning to trust Him completely. He had set the stage perfectly by forming a beautiful team relationship between my parents and me. I didn't have to walk this path alone! I had two people who dearly loved me and wanted the best for me, and who were committed to seeking God with me and supporting me every step of the way!

It was incredible how God wrote each line of our love story just at the perfect time. Little did I know how important that conversation with my parents would be to the rest of the script.

Honoring our parents can sweeten our love story!

Believe me, I never would have thought that adding parents to the picture could possibly bring *romance*. But some of the most unforgettably romantic moments in my love story with Eric involved our parents...

Eric and I had a close friendship for many months before anything romantic happened between us. In fact, neither one of us would have ever expected a relationship to develop, because we were five years apart in age and I saw him as a godly older brother. But there came a point where we both began to ponder some questions about our friendship. Even if we *were* "just friends," was it possible we were spending too much time together? Individually, we both had committed to God that even our friendships with the opposite sex would be completely pure and honoring to our future marriage partner. Now we wondered if our future spouses came into our lives, would they be comfortable with how much time we were spending together?

One summer day, while riding in a van together on the way home from a short-term mission outreach to inner city New Orleans, Eric brought up the subject.

"I want to honor and respect my future wife, and *your* future husband," he began. "My friendship with you is so important to me, but sometimes I wonder if we are *too* close. Maybe we are spending too much time together. It might be good for us to spend some time apart, praying about this."

As I nodded my head in agreement, Eric made another unexpected statement. "And maybe I should get together with your dad."

Without thinking I replied, "Yeah, I think you should."

There was a moment of strained silence as we pondered our verbal mishaps. We were each wondering why in the world we had agreed that Eric should talk to my dad. It wasn't as if he was going to ask for my hand in marriage or anything! We felt too foolish to bring it up again, however.

We soon found out that God knew exactly what He was doing in guiding our conversation along those lines. A few days later, Eric met my dad for lunch at a nearby restaurant. Eric nervously sipped his water as my dad studied the menu.

Why am I doing this? What am I even going to say? Eric wondered for the hundredth time. However, he was here, and he was going to make the best of it. Once they had ordered, Eric took a deep breath and began his prepared speech.

"Rich, um, I just wanted to talk to you about my friendship with Leslie," he started as my dad calmly gazed across the table at him. He swallowed awkwardly, then continued.

"I mean, I just want to be careful. Leslie and I are spending a lot of time together, and I want to honor her future husband and my future wife in this whole thing. I'm just wondering if you have any suggestions for how much time we should be spending together."

My dad was silent a moment or two. Then he began to share a few words of wisdom that Eric would never forget.

"Eric, one of the reasons I know your friendship with Leslie is from God," he said confidently, "is because ever since you have been in her life, I've seen her only draw closer to God as a result of the friendship."

One of the beautiful things about having teammates is that they provide an outside perspective on a friendship or a relationship. They can see things that we are sometimes blinded to. Our teammates can help us determine whether or not a relationship is from God *based on the fruit they see in our lives as a result of the relationship.* If the relationship is drawing us away from God and other priorities, we need to seriously re-evaluate things. However, if the friendship or relationship is drawing us closer to God and producing godly fruit in our lives, that is a way of knowing that it might be something God Himself has put together.

Our teammates can see our life from the outside, and therefore help us discern what is really going on. My parents had observed what positive fruit my friendship with Eric had created in my life. They were able to clearly see that Eric had inspired and encouraged me to have even a deeper love and passion for the Lord.

With my dad's insightful words, Eric realized all the more, the value of having strong godly mentors such as our parents to come to with questions such as the ones he had burning on his heart. My dad wasn't finished imparting timeless wisdom, however. His next phrase startled Eric, but taught him an incredible truth.

"Eric," my dad continued, "I *know* your relationship with my daughter is pure." Then he paused as Eric pondered how he could be so confident of that fact without being around us twenty-four hours a day. As if reading his thoughts, my dad answered his question. "If your relationship with Leslie wasn't pure," he said, "God would tell me."

At such a bold statement Eric's heart nearly stopped. *God* would tell him? At that moment Eric was nearly weak with relief that our friendship had indeed been pure. He could just imagine how terrible it would be to have God wake my dad up in the night to tell him that it *wasn't* pure! Eric pictured this irate father chasing him down the street with a shotgun!

After he got over the shock of what my dad had just told him, Eric suddenly realized a profound truth. He had always thought of me as an individual, independent and making all my own decisions. Yet now he realized that God had put a protective covering over my life—the authority of my parents. God had given me as a treasure to my parents for them to care for me, provide for me, and protect me. In that flash of realization, he saw how very wrong it would be for him to ever pursue a romantic relationship with me without first honoring the position God had given my parents.

From that moment on, Eric decided that *his* parents as well as his future wife's parents were going to be involved in the relationship from the beginning. He made a silent commitment to honor and *respect* the parents' authority over his own life as well as over the girl he would marry.

Before he could ponder these new thoughts any longer, my dad began speaking again, this time shocking Eric even more.

"And Eric, I just want you to know that Janet and I give you our blessing to pursue a relationship with our daughter in any way God would lead you."

Eric stared at him a moment. Had Rich misunderstood his intentions? He tried to clarify. "Rich, actually, that's *not* what I'm after at all…"

My dad held up his hand to interrupt. "I know," he replied gently, "but for some reason, I just felt like I should give you that freedom."

Romance and Respect

Through an amazing series of events, it was only a few weeks later that Eric became sure that I was the one he would marry someday.

Eric was true to his commitment to honor and respect my parent's position in my life. He decided, after much prayer, to discuss this with my dad before talking to me about it. He had a pretty good idea of my feelings toward him, and he knew my dad would know better than anyone where I stood.

He found himself again sitting across the table from my dad at the same restaurant, this time early in the morning before work. But now, he *knew* what he had come to say. As my dad sipped his coffee and tried to wake up, Eric dove right into the purpose of this meeting.

"Rich, after praying a lot about my friendship with Leslie over the past few weeks, I feel that God has shown me that one day Leslie is going to be my wife."

Needless to say, my dad woke up quickly! But after a moment's recovery, he gave an amazing response.

"Eric," he said, looking him straight in the eye, "Janet and I have been praying for Leslie's future husband since the day we became Christians fourteen years ago. We prayed that we would recognize him when he came into her life. And, Eric, we've known for some time that *you* are the one."

What incredible confirmation! Eric was full of gratitude that God had allowed him to "make the mistake" of getting together with my dad to discuss his friendship with me. He was a young man who felt he was often blundering his way through life, especially when it came to the area of relationships. It felt so wonderful to now have a teammate in the most unexpected person—his future father-in-law!

As for me, when I found out all this had happened, it deepened my appreciation for this man named Eric Ludy. By the time this conversation took place, my heart was telling me that someday I would marry him. And now I realized all the more what a true man of integrity he was. That he would respect me enough to honor my parents in approaching our relationship—this was true romance!

A few days later, my dad gave Eric the ultimate compliment. "Eric," he said smiling, "I give you my blessing to win my daughter's heart."

When my dad gave Eric the blessing to "win my heart," he didn't just leave it there. After the relationship began, Eric and my dad met together on a regular basis...and my dad taught him *how* to win my heart. My dad was the man who knew me better than any other man in the world. And now he was passing his knowledge about me along to the man I would spend the rest of my life with!

When I realized this was going on, I was instantly transformed into a princess. I felt *so* cherished! The two most important men in my life were spending hours doing nothing but discussing who I was, how I was made, how they could understand me better, and more than anything, how they could *love me!* Don't try to tell me that's not incredibly romantic! What girl wouldn't feel adored and treasured with something so special taking place in her life?

When I saw how committed Eric was to learning how to be sensitive to me and how determined he was to honor and respect my parents...my respect for *him* only grew. I knew without a doubt he was the kind of man with whom I wanted to spend my life.

My parents were wonderful teammates. The months and years that followed built a bond between us that I never knew was possible. They showed their love to me in amazing ways—late night talks and prayer sessions, little notes of encouragement, and doing everything they could to help make my relationship with Eric special. They even helped Eric coordinate the details of the night he proposed to me!

Eric and I chose to invite our parents to be our teammates as God scripted our love story. It was one of the best decisions we ever made. Not only did it add excitement and romance to our relationship in ways we never could have dreamed of, it also provided the strength and outside perspective we needed to make our love story successful. While Eric and I had the leading roles, the Great Author of romance had cast the perfect supporting characters—we couldn't have played our parts without them!

When Parents Aren't in the Picture

When Eric and I share about our parents being involved in our love story, we often hear the comment, "Yeah, but who has parents like that? I think *that* part of your love story is a little too good for regular people who have messed up families."

It is tragic that most people are not blessed with loving and God-fearing parents. In a world where divorce, abuse, and abandonment run rampant, I must admit that healthy families are becoming the exception rather than the rule. If your family is not what it should be, if your parents are not walking with the Lord, or maybe not even alive anymore, it's still important to have godly teammates. And there *is* hope even when parents aren't able or willing to join our team.

The beauty of God's ways cannot be limited to mere circumstance. He promises to be a "Father to the fatherless" (Psalm 68:5). His loving heart goes out with compassion to those with parents who don't know how to love their children.

The beauty of the Body of Christ is that whether or not we have a biological family, we have a spiritual family all around us. God can provide special people in your life to fill the position that your parents can't.

Just take a closer look at the ones who give you the most support—your pastor, your grandmother, or a godly mentor. Those people love you. Just as you could go to your parents and invite them to help you seek God in your love life, so you can go to them with the same request. Most likely they will be honored and take their position as your teammate quite seriously.

Even if you are separated from your parents by geography, it's important to have teammates nearby with whom you can walk through the journey of your relationship on a day to day basis. God is faithful to provide this type of support as well.

Amanda, a twenty-six-year-old exchange student from Canada, found herself in England, miles away from her parents, when a young man came into her life whom she was drawn to.

"My parents were supportive in prayer for me, but I still needed someone to help me walk through the day to day stuff. Someone to whom I could make myself accountable, and who could observe my relationship with this man on a regular basis," she told me. "I finally asked God to provide a father-figure and a mother-figure for me who could help me through the process of discerning God's will in this relationship."

God led her to her pastor and his wife, a kindly older couple who had learned to love Amanda like a daughter. They eagerly joined her in prayer about the young man in her life. When they felt they had wisdom to share with her, they did. They were with her each step of the way as the relationship grew towards marriage.

"It was wonderful!" Amanda recalls, "God provided exactly what I needed through this couple. And the best part was that my pastor actually performed the wedding ceremony! God is so faithful!"

No matter what kind of parents you have, God loves you like a faithful Father. He wants the best for you, and He will never let you down.

Playing to Win

Even though we live in a "do-it-yourself" world, it is dangerous to take that attitude toward relationships. The decision of who to spend the rest of our life with is a choice that has repercussions which will last for as long as we live. It's not a choice we should take lightly. And it's not a decision we should make alone.

Even if we are seeking God, it's wise to invite other perspectives into the picture. Not because God isn't capable of leading and guiding, but because we aren't always capable of listening and making the wisest choices on our own. As the writer of Proverbs eloquently reminds us:

> *Plans fail for lack of counsel, but with many advisers they succeed.*
>
> 15:22 NIV

But be warned—choose your teammates wisely. Just as godly input can help make a relationship successful, the wrong kind of counselors can lead to disaster.

Jeff, a nineteen-year-old computer whiz, noticed a beautiful young woman at his church who had a genuine heart for God. As he built a friendship with her, he began to feel strongly that she might be the one he was to marry.

He prayed for awhile about pursuing a relationship with her, but he was too stubborn to ask anyone else for advice on the subject, especially his parents. Though they were full of wisdom and loved him, he was out to prove that he could "hear God" on his own. He did ask a couple of his rather shallow "Christian" friends for their opinions. "Go for it, man," they all said confidently without much thought. So Jeff dove headfirst into the relationship, but it soon exploded in his face. He hadn't taken time to have anyone pray with him or give him an outside perspective. He pursued things far too quickly and scared the poor girl away. Jeff deeply regrets his approach.

"It could have turned out wonderfully, if I had just listened to the people in my life who really have wisdom," he recalls miserably. "But I was so intent on doing things my own way that I ruined it. The few people I did ask for advice weren't really even qualified to give it."

Those people in your life who dearly love you and care about you, who are older, wiser, and have a lifetime of godly fruit to back up their words are the best teammates you can pick. Who are the supporting characters God may be casting in your love story? You don't need to wait until a relationship comes into your life to invite them to be on your team. From the time I was about twelve-years-old, a dear Christian couple who had been friends of our family for years began to faithfully pray for my future husband. Besides having my parents to turn to if I needed support, I also went to them from time to time to ask for prayer about specific situations. Thanks to God's provision, my teammates—my loving parents as well as other godly mentors—were in place long before my love story began.

When it comes to our love life, we're talking about one of the most important decisions we'll ever make...so let's play to win.

A Step Further

Take a few minutes and read over a few wise tidbits from one of the smartest guys who ever lived. These timeless truths are all found in the book of Proverbs: 12:15, 15:22, 19:20, 20:18, 24:6, and 27:9. Let this wisdom sink deep into your mind and learn to live by it. You might even want to knock on your parent's door and extend to them the invitation to officially join your team!

Section Five

Discovering a God-Written Love Story

Chapter Fifteen

Leslie:
Too Late?

*A glimmer of hope
in a world of lost virginity*

Her name was Rebecca. She was a gentle, dark-haired beauty who had not yet reached thirteen. Her blossoming figure and striking face caused her to look older than her years…but inwardly she was still a child, only just beginning to embark upon the confusing journey into womanhood.

At church and at school, boys began to notice her. Boys who had not yet matured out of childhood, but who desperately wanted to be seen as men. Rebecca began to gain a sense of being loved and accepted through the attention of these young men—a love she had failed to receive from her parents growing up.

She met Jason at youth group. He was a good-looking, confident sixteen-year-old. Whenever he smiled at her from across the room, she felt something inside of her leap. Soon he was sitting with her every week, treating her as a protective and caring older brother. Her child's heart embraced the sense of security and warmth he brought to her, while the *woman* she was becoming began to feel a new and exciting attraction to him. As the weeks passed, her infatuation grew, as did her complete trust in this charming young man.

One night Jason invited Rebecca over to his house while his parents were out of town. Rebecca entered Jason's home as an innocent child of twelve, but hours later she left as a used and defiled sex toy. Overnight Rebecca was forced from childhood into womanhood—but in the most unnatural and heart-wrenching way imaginable. She had lost her virginity before she had even fully developed physically or emotionally.

Rebecca was devastated and confused. Jason was finished with her and on to new prey. God's heart was breaking for Rebecca and Jason.

Todd was an outgoing pre-med student at a Christian college in California. He had a deep love for the Lord and a passion to serve others. In spite of his heavy class load, Todd was actively involved in several campus ministries. He also led worship once a week at his local church. His long-term dream was to become a medical missionary.

He met Karly at an early morning prayer meeting he was leading. She was attractive, funny, and intelligent. Todd was fascinated by her. They met for coffee and ended up talking for three hours. From that day on, they were rarely apart. Drawn together by their mutual love for the Lord and a desire to go on the mission field together, they became an inseparable pair. Within two months, they knew someday they would be married, and they even began to talk seriously about engagement. All their fellow believers looked up to them as a wonderful example of a godly relationship.

One evening, passion unexpectedly overcame common sense, and the next thing they knew they were waking up in bed together…stunned by what they had allowed themselves to do.

Suddenly their beautiful, exciting relationship became awkward and strained. Their joy in talking about the Lord vanished. Their mutual passion for the mission field faded as well. Todd was riddled with gut-wrenching shame. For the first time in his life, he felt like a failure. He was no longer a confident student and Christian leader. He felt unworthy of God's love and unqualified for leadership. He dropped out of all his church activities. He pulled away from friendships. His grades began to slip. He fell into a deep depression, feeling as if he'd ruined not only his life and future, but Karly's as well.

As for Karly, she was hurt and confused by Todd's behavior. She had thought he loved her. She had made the mistake of giving him her most precious gift—her virginity, but now he was distant and cold toward her. She was full of guilt. When she thought of all her childhood dreams of walking down the aisle in a white wedding gown—symbolizing her purity—she felt sick. She could never hope to have a beautiful love story with Todd now. She had ruined her chance. She was inwardly miserable, and had no one to talk to about her pain.

God's heart was breaking for Todd and Karly.

Sin Is Serious

Sexual sin…impurity…moral compromise. In any form, in any circumstance, its effects are devastating. Sin rips lives and hearts apart—destroying innocence, beauty, and joy. Sin's consequences often follow us for the rest of our lifetime, and sometimes even the next generation must pay the price for the mess we have made of our lives.

The most damaging result of sin is that it pushes us away from our Creator. We carry the guilt of what we've done in our hearts—attempting to keep it hidden from Him, and then we end up wandering helplessly and alone, miles away from the One who loves us.

Growing up in Christian circles, I often observed the issue of sexual sin being treated lightly. In some youth groups I belonged to, it was *expected* that most of us would give away our virginity before we got married. The attitude was, "You are all going to mess up in this area, because in this day and age, sexual sin is nearly inevitable. But don't worry, God offers a second virginity. His grace will cover you."

There is some truth to that statement. Yes, we will all make mistakes, but this does not mean it is inevitable that we will all fall into sexual sin, or that purity is impossible, and that we are just a "victim of the culture" if we cannot achieve it. Yes, God *does* offer grace and forgiveness, and He *can* give us a "second virginity," spiritually speaking. But we should never take advantage of His wonderful grace. And we should never treat our sin lightly. In the eyes of a holy God, our sin is detestable.

When Eric was a young zealous fireball, traveling the world as a missionary, he was asked to speak to a large youth event in Virginia. As he prayed before the meeting, he felt that God wanted him to speak about purity—spiritual, emotional, and physical. During his talk, he exhorted the young people to live according to God's standards for purity, rather than imitating the culture around them. He talked about physical purity, mental purity, and emotional purity. His message was convicting and powerful. And the church leaders did not like it. A youth pastor got up immediately after Eric finished speaking and took the microphone.

"Well, *I'm* not going to preach to you about *holiness*," he said apologetically, as if preaching "holiness" was as distasteful and inappropriate as giving a lecture on parasite removal from the large intestine.

Afterwards a group of leaders confronted Eric.

"Eric, how dare you make all these kids feel condemned? Almost all of them have blown it in the area of purity! It's too sensitive a subject for you to speak about purity that way. Now they are going to feel *guilty!* You better get back up there and ask their forgiveness!"

When we take this attitude toward sexual sin—that it's just a little mistake most of us make and that we shouldn't get too hung up over it—we deny the awesome and amazing power of what Christ did for us on the cross. In truth, sexual sin is horrifying. It breaks the heart of God. It destroys that natural perfect order of love that God created between a man and woman. It violates us. We *should* feel remorse when we sin in this way...and we should realize the *gravity* of what we have done. And yet, that's not where it should end.

Once, after a seminar in Australia, I knelt to pray with a young woman about twenty-five, who was weeping uncontrollably. Her petite body shook with heart-wrenching sobs. I prayed for God's peace to comfort her heart. As she began to calm down, she haltingly told me what her burden was.

"I have given away the most precious thing I had—my purity. There's nothing left of my treasure. How could I do such a thing? The guy I gave myself to didn't even love me. Now I have nothing to offer my husband. It's too late for me. God doesn't want to waste His time with me anymore. I've ruined my whole life."

Yet before the evening was over, this young woman had an encounter with the grace of God, and she was changed. Her face became radiant and peaceful. She knew she was forgiven.

Another time after a speaking event in Texas, I met a young woman who was nearly numb with guilt and horror over what she had done. Not only had she compromised herself sexually...she'd had an abortion. Her eyes were hollow with pain. Yet as she came face to face with her God that day, she became new. As she left, there was a bright sparkle in her eyes. She could begin to move on with her life and discover all God had for her. She knew she was forgiven.

His Tender Smile

The beauty of a God-written love story is not something reserved for the perfect and pious—it's for the sinners like you and like me. That's what God's love is all about. We are so unworthy of His grace and forgiveness—and yet He offers it to us freely. If you have fallen in this area of your life and have asked yourself the question, "Is it too late for me?" then let the following story from Scripture show you Jesus' heart for *you,* a sinner.

Jesus went to the Mount of Olives. At dawn He came back to the temple, and all the people came to Him. Just as He sat down to teach, the scribes and Pharisees led in a woman who had been caught committing adultery. They made her stand in the middle of everyone.

"Teacher," they said to Him, "this woman has been caught in the very act of committing adultery. In the Law, Moses commanded to stone this kind of woman. What do You say?"...

But Jesus knelt and wrote down something on the ground. As they continued questioning Him, He straightened up and said to them, "The one among you who is without sin, let him throw the first stone at her.'

Again, He knelt and wrote down something on the ground. Those who heard left one at a time, beginning with the older ones first, leaving Jesus alone with the woman.[1]

How did Jesus look at the woman who had broken His heart by her sin? In his book, *The Parable of Joy*, Michael Card beautifully describes the way Jesus responded to the woman at that moment. The following scene is a perfect portrayal of the tender heart of the Shepherd toward His little lost lambs.

She was standing alone, shivering, in front of the man who was just getting to His feet.

"Where did everyone go?" He asked, smiling, "Didn't anyone condemn you?"

"No," she whispered, looking down. "No one, Sir."

He took her chin in one of His hands. 'I don't condemn you either,' He said with a tender smile.

Then He became serious. He spoke as a parent disciplining a child. "Now go, and stop sinning."

She began to weep, not from shame as before, but from relief. He had saved her life. He had returned to her what the others...had stolen. She was sorry, painfully sorry. At last she had found Someone who could bear her sorrow for her.[2]

In *The Parable of Joy*, Michael Card notes that a commentator named Frederick Buechner once said of Jesus' response to the woman caught in adultery, "He did not condemn her, because He would be condemned *for* her."[3]

Just as Jesus knew the sins of each person in that crowd, He knows every sin we have ever committed from the day we were born. It is foolish to try to keep our sins hidden from Him. Yet when we come to Him, bleeding and broken, filled with pain and regret, afraid of His anger, and look into His eyes...He smiles tenderly. He lifts our chin with His nail-scarred hand. And He gently says, "I don't condemn you. Now go, and stop sinning."

When we come face to face with this perfect love, it takes our breath away. We deserve to die for what we have done. We should be stoned by an angry mob. But not only does Jesus save our life with His own blood, He washes us *completely* clean. When He looks at us, He doesn't see our failures and mistakes, He sees a new creation—a child of God.

He exhorts us "to go and stop sinning." He is speaking of repentance. This is the act of humbling ourselves, confessing our sin, and determining in our heart to turn and walk away from our sin from this day forward. Repentance literally means *turning from our sin and walking the other direction.* And with His tender guiding hand in our lives, we can repent…and be made new. When we repent and accept His forgiveness, He can take the sin that our enemy meant to use to destroy us, and use it for His glory. He can take a shattered heart and life and script a beautiful tale of His perfect love.

The Power to Forgive

Sexual sin causes pain. To move on to the beautiful plans God has for our lives, we must get past the crippling effects of unforgiveness. Todd cannot forgive himself for falling into sin. Karly cannot forgive herself *or* Todd for allowing this to happen. As Rachel grows older she will struggle to forgive Jason for taking advantage of her vulnerable heart and defiling her at the age of twelve.

When we come face to face with the tender, forgiving eyes of our Redeemer, only then will we gain the power to forgive ourselves—and those who have used us. In light of the forgiveness Christ has offered us, how can we offer less to those who have hurt us? They are only sinners like us.

If you have been devastated by sin, riddled with guilt over your mistakes, overcome with bitterness towards someone who has used you, it's time to run into the arms of Jesus and look into His loving eyes. Allow Him to wash you clean, white as snow, and give you a fresh start. His plans for you are more amazing than you can imagine. A God-written love story maybe just on the horizon for you! Allow Him to remove the song of loneliness and remorse you have been singing, and to place into your heart a new song—the "sweeter song."

White As Snow

These are song lyrics from our album "Heavenly Perspective." It's a melody dedicated to anyone who has felt the pain of losing a precious treasure of purity. Through these words, may God bathe your heart with His perfect love and give you new vision and hope for the future.

Alone and confused, your heart is bruised from
*   sin;.*
Your joy is gone from love gone wrong
And you're longing to start again.
I know that you've been hurt, and you don't
*   know whom to trust;*
I won't pretend I understand your pain.
But I can see repentance in your eyes, and I
*   know it's not too late;*
I hear Him calling your name...

White as snow, He has made you white as snow;
The moment you confessed, His heart forgave.
You might think you've ruined all the plans He
*   had for you,*
But it's for that very reason Jesus saves.
White as snow, He has made you white as snow;
Pure and innocent like a dove,
Though you have done nothing to deserve His
*   pardoning,*
You've been purified by Jesus blood—
White as snow

The guilt and the shame, keeping you chained,
Not wanting to let you go;
It's not how you dreamed, not how you planned,
And you can't see that still there is hope.

Receive His healing for your bruises;
Receive His riches for your rages.
You cannot imagine all the plans He has for you,
So take His hand, and don't look back.

A Step Further

Quietly steal away and kneel before the throne of God.
Read through Psalm 51, and let the words of David begging
for forgiveness to his Lord become the cry of your heart to
God. Then read Luke 15:11-24 and let yourself go on a journey with the wayward son. Allow the loving and welcoming
arms of your Father enfold you and take you back once again.

> *Leave the Irreparable Past in His hands,*
> *and step out into the Irresistible Future with*
> *Him.*[4]

Oswald Chambers

Chapter Sixteen

Eric:
Against the Tide

*Gaining real backbone in
the midst of a spineless generation*

A Thin Blanket

The night air was cold, frigid cold! In the icy prison cell sat two young Chinese men, emaciated from loss of food and light. They both had only a thin blanket to keep them warm.

The hard floor beneath them was cruel and merciless, and the shackles upon their ankles seemed to mock their pain. Yet in this arctic sanctuary of doom was heavenly warmth.

One of the two young men had a thought.

If that were Jesus next to me, would I give Him my blanket?

This Chinese man who had but a thin blanket to keep himself warm, recognized the privilege it would be to give what little he had to the God who had given him *everything*. He removed the blanket from around his shoulders and placed it around the shoulders of his shivering friend.

Our Blanket, Our Life

I want you to picture yourself in the same, icy cold prison cell. Imagine that you are thin and frail and trembling from the cold. And all you have is a thin blanket to warm yourself. How tightly would you cling to the little comfort you have? What would it take for you to part with your precious blanket?

You see, that thin blanket represents our life. If we give up our blanket, we're going to die. If we let go of our lone security, we must surrender to death.

But what if the one next to you in that cell was Jesus? What if you had the privilege of giving what little you had to the one who gave up His life for you? What if you *really did* have the opportunity to show your love and gratitude to the King of all Kings and the Creator of the Universe? Would *you* give up your blanket?

As a generation, we have been taught to hold onto our blankets, to secure our future even at the expense of those around us. But we fail to realize that the security of our future rests *not* in our blanket, *but in Jesus* sitting next to us. When we choose to give instead of keep, we discover a little taste of heaven on earth. When we choose to let go of what little we have and surrender it to God, it's then we receive the bounty of His kingdom.

Our love-hungry generation is desperately searching for the "beautiful side of love." But it is not found in either sexual intercourse or abstinence from sexual intercourse. The "sweeter song" *is* Jesus, in all His fullness, all His love, all His beauty, all His grace, and all His majesty.

When you know Jesus Christ, the tender hand of heaven begins to masterfully shape your life to exhibit the glory of heaven for the entire world to see. When you know the Great Author of romance, the tender hand of heaven takes you by the heart and trains you to love as the Great Lover Himself. He trains you to be patient and pure. He trains you to be tender and true. With Jesus at the center of your life, you not only gain blissful hope for the here and now, but unquenchable excitement for the eternity before you.

The "sweeter song" is sung on a ship that is headed against the tide. Its course is charted to go directly into the headwinds. Jesus plays the sweetest melody men's ears have ever heard, but you need backbone to board the ship on which it is played.

Many churches today are using the slogan "Christianity is *cool*" as their drawing card, thinking that maybe more people would be Christians if they knew that churches weren't full of brainless idiots who lean on God as a crutch, because they can't handle life's problems on their own. Well, *in heaven,* Christianity is cool, but here on earth, Christianity is anything *but* cool. True Christianity throughout history has been mocked and ridiculed, persecuted and even killed by the world around. In fact, if anyone chooses to truly live like Christ in this world, he will undoubtedly meet the same fate…the cross.

Christianity is not the *easy* way to pass through this life. To hear the tender melody line of the "sweeter song," *there is a sacrifice!* Often times it means losing a reputation, being misunderstood by the masses…or even giving up your thin blanket.

I have a vision for our generation of Christians. I want to see us go beyond Sunday morning services and Wednesday night Bible studies—and learn to love Christ in every minute of every day. I want to see us go beyond just memorizing Scripture and knowing the verbiage of the Bible—to actually having our lives transformed by its amazing Truth, so that we don't just *know it,* but we *live it* for all the world to witness. I want to see us fight to gain back the "beautiful side of love" in our romantic relationships, so that we can bring glory to the Great Lover of our souls.

Many have commented on how our generation lacks leaders. And many have said that if our generation doesn't change its course, it's headed straight for the rocks upon which the Sirens sit. And unfortunately, I would have to agree. We are a dying, spineless generation. We lack the courage to stand for anything that's politically and socially incorrect. We lack the faith to trust that God is as perfect and powerful as He says He is. We lack the fire to *pursue* God, the zeal to *know* God, and the humility to *allow* God to do whatsoever He pleases with our lives.

We are a generation inundated with sexual perversity, overwhelmed with relational infidelity, and riddled with a catastrophic divorce rate whose growth curve seems to have only just begun. When I think about our generation and how desperately we need young leaders to stand up, I am reminded of a heroic tale that unfolded on the Judean countryside many thousands of years ago.

Seeing Beyond the Hulk

All hope seemed lost! The odds makers in Las Vegas were heavily favoring the Champion. I mean, who could possibly beat *him!* He was huge! He was stronger than an ox and bigger than a small dinosaur. His biceps alone could have housed a small family. Not only that, but he had the attitude needed to win a fight like this one. Sports writers today call it "cocky"; back then they just called it, "Whoa, Momma! I'm not gonna fight this dude!"

The ring was not in Caesar's Palace, but actually in a less glittery venue called the Valley of Elah. And this wasn't a fight to the ten count, but *a fight to the death*. This wasn't a fight for fame, but a fight for the future of a nation. This showdown was one for the history books before the bell even rang.

Each nation chose their fighter. It was the "Hulk," weighing in at five hundred pounds plus and able to swallow a baby tiger with a single gulp, against the "Kid," a young sheepherder, about the same size as the Champion's left leg. The "Hulk" howled with laughter as he saw the "Kid" stroll out to fight.

If a nation's future hung in the balance, why choose a young shepherd boy to fight for you? Why not pick your greatest warrior to match strength with the champion? The odds were already a million to one. Why make them even worse?

Well, *this* nation picked their fighter, not based on public-opinion polls or in alignment with Las Vegas odds. They picked their fighter because he was the only one willing to fight. Every other warrior was quaking in his combat boots.

But don't judge this "Kid" on his external size and physical prowess. This "Kid" was special! He knew something that every other warrior in his entire nation didn't know. He knew that if you stand up for God, He stands up for you.

The "Hulk" was mocking God and His people. Only this unimpressive "Kid" seemed to notice that *that* was a big time no-no. So he said, "I'll take him on!"

I'm convinced that when the "Kid" strolled out to meet the "Hulk" that day, it wasn't the awesome size, the impenetrable strength, and the death-defying confidence of the giant he saw. I believe he saw his infinitely enormous and all-powerful God standing behind the scrawny giant, with His gargantuan fist over the "Hulk's" miniscule head, saying to the young shepherd, "Just tell me when! (CRUNCH!!)"

The "Kid's" name was David. And he was a leader in a generation that only had eyes for the "Hulk" named Goliath (1 Samuel 17). He was fearless amid a generation that trembled with fear. And he was a man of backbone, when all around him his peers were spineless.

We desperately need Davids in our generation. We need leaders who will trust God implicitly. We need men and women who will stand up against the "hulks" in our culture and not back down. We need heroes who will not pattern themselves after the fearful throng around them, but pattern themselves after the courage of Christ.

Our generation needs ordinary people who choose to love God in extraordinary ways. We need a new batch of leaders in this world who place more value on dying for the sake of Truth, than on living to get re-elected. We need a generation of lovers who ask, "What would Jesus do?" and then *really do it!*

> *You've trusted Jesus with your life, now live that life in Him. Inhaling Him. Exhaling Him. Making Him your life-source each and every day with the faith of a little child! You were planted in the richest of soils and watered with the amazing Truth of His Kingdom. Don't hide the joy-filled life of Jesus beneath the soil, but grow and bloom for all the world to see.*

Colossians 2:7 (paraphrase)

How 'Bout Your Blanket?

Join me, once again, in that icy prison cell. Place yourself on that mercilessly hard floor, and remember that you are frigidly cold. It's that thin blanket that represents your only comfort, your only blockade from the deathly chill.

Imagine that it is not a young Chinese man who sits shivering next to you, but it is *your future spouse*. Ask yourself the question,

"If that were Jesus seated next to me, would I give Him my blanket?"

As you ponder how you would respond, maybe you hold up your blanket and see that it is tattered and torn. Maybe you don't even have a blanket left, and all that remains is a mere thread that drapes itself across your heart, attempting to protect you from the bitter cold.

Many of us don't even have much of a blanket to offer our spouse who shivering beside us. But, if we were to see them as Jesus, would we be willing to give the *little* we do have to the God who gave us so much?

Extravagant love, as in every generation before us, has been ridiculed and scorned. It is seen as a waste and a reckless overspending. But extravagant love, the offering of everything, the emptying of the pockets of our life, is the essence of true Christianity. It was extravagant love that caused Jesus to give up His throne in heaven, and give us the gift of life at the expense of His own life. It was extravagant love that compelled the Chinese Christian to sacrifice his only source of warmth for the benefit of his brother in prison. And it would be extravagant love that would cause you to take the blanket off your shoulders today and wrap it around the shoulders of your Worthy King.

If you allow the tender hand of heaven to pour this kind of extravagant love into your heart, then you will truly be ready to be a successful lover. With an extravagant love stirring in your every attitude and action, it is fairly certain you will not be applauded by this world, but the heavenly hosts will be on their feet cheering, as you model the "beautiful side of love" for the entire universe to watch.

When you entrust the "pen" of your life to the Great Author of romance and learn how to love with extravagance, you won't just be humming the praises of God for a lifetime, but you will be singing the "sweeter song" for all eternity!

Wet Eyes

Wet eyes are watching you. The moist eyes of Jesus, tenderly longing for you to let go of your life and hold fast to Him. His eyes are gentle as they see you stumble and scrape your knee in sin once again. He doesn't kick you when you're down, but rather He carefully stabilizes you with His mercy and grace, and helps you to your feet. He is so patient when you falter, and is ever faithful to forgive you.

His eyes are smiling as they find you longing to please Him. Just as the little three-year-old child picks up a crayon and scribbles a masterpiece for his earthly father, so you scribble your very best rendition of a life honoring to your Father in heaven. And even though He might not be able to tell if it is a picture of Him or a hippo, your little scribbles of love mean everything to your God.

His eyes are also full of pride as they observe you trusting Him. He, more than anyone, knows how difficult it is to stand against the tide. He simply wants an ordinary person to trust His nature and character, and to test His perfect faithfulness. And, as Oswald Chambers has said,

"If we deliberately choose to obey God, then He will tax the remotest star and the last grain of sand to assist us with all His almighty power."[1]

Wet eyes are watching you. The caring eyes of heaven have spent too many years burning with tears of pain over your life and mine. Let us choose today to bless God's heart with the gift of loving Him with all our heart, soul, mind, and strength. Let's make those wet eyes proud!

A Final Challenge

Our loving Savior and Lord has given us an amazing opportunity—to rise above the watered-down version of love this world offers us and take hold of the truest and most lasting kind of love imaginable. It's a chance to set aside Hollywood's sappy standards and discover romance at its best...the romance of heaven! It's time to make a choice. We can embrace an empty, selfish lifestyle that ends in heartache and despair, or we can learn to live and love selflessly...just like our own Great Lover Himself.

God is longing to write *your* love story—a love story far beyond the most incredible fairy-tale ever written. Will you give Him the pen today?

You cannot stay the way you are and go with God.[2]

Henry Blackabee

God has ventured all in Jesus Christ to save us, now He wants us to venture our all in abandoned confidence in Him.[3]

Oswald Chambers

Be assured, if you walk with Him and look to Him and expect help from Him, He will never fail you.[4]

George Mueller

The thing that taxes almightiness is the very thing which we as disciples of Jesus ought to believe He will do.[5]
Oswald Chambers

The man who has God for his treasure has all things in One.[6]

A.W. Tozer

A Step Further

Sit down, take your time, and read through the amazing account in Daniel 6: 4-23. Then go on a little stroll and invite Jesus to come along. As you walk, ponder the world in which you live. God has placed you upon this earth for such a time as this. Let this day be a turning point in your life—a decision to stand against the tide for His Truth. You cannot stand in your own strength, but if you remember the enormous God backing you up, you will be filled with true courage to face the lions. He will never leave you (Hebrews 13:5).

Notes

Chapter 2

1. Richard Lattimore, *Homer's Odyssey* (New York: Harper and Row Publishers, Inc., 1950), 189-190.
2. Facts on File Encyclopedia of World Mythology and Legend, s. v. "Orpheus."

Chapter 3

1. John Foxe, *Foxe's Book of Martyrs* (Grand Rapids, Mich.: Baker Book House, 1990), 7-8.
2. Elisabeth Elliot, *Shadow of the Almighty: The Life and Testament of Jim Elliot*, (San Francisco: HarperCollins, 1979), 15.
3. Mrs. Charles E. Cowman, *Streams in the Desert* (Grand Rapids, Mich.: Zondervan Publishing House, 1984), 31. Used by permission of OMS International, Inc., P.O. Box A, Greenwood. Ind. 46142-6599.

Chapter 4

1. Oswald Chambers, *My Utmost for His Highest* (Uhrichsville, Ohio: Barbour Publishing, Inc., 1935), 37. This material is taken from *My Utmost for His Highest* by Oswald Chambers. Copyright © 1935 by Doug Mead & Co., renewed © 1963 by the Oswald Chambers Publications Assn. Ltd., and is used by permission of Discovery House Publishers, Box 3566, Grand Rapids, MI 49501. All rights reserved.
2. Ibid., 58.
3. Elisabeth Elliot, *A Chance to Die* (Grand Rapids, Mich.: Fleming H. Revell, 1987), 31.
4. Chambers, 73.

Chapter 5

1. Richard Wurmbrandt, *If that were Christ would you give him your blanket?* (Middlebury, Ind.: Living Sacrifice Books, 1970), 2. For more information on today's persecuted church, call The Voice of Martyrs at (918) 337-8015.
2. Richard Wurmbrandt, "Give a Gem at Christmas," *Voice of the Martyrs,* December, 1998. For more information on today's persecuted church, call The Voice of Martyrs at (918) 337-8015.

Chapter 6

1. Chuck Colson, "Any Old World View Will Do," *Perspective,* May, 1998.

Chapter 9

1. Lattimore, 305-328.
2. Chambers, 129.
3. Cowman, 195.

Chapter 10

1. Cowman, 33.
2. From a lecture given by Elisabeth Elliot.
3. Amy Grant, "I Love a Lonely Day," *Age to Age* (Waco, Tex.: Myrrh, 1982).
4. Cowman, 216.

Chapter 11

1. Source unknown.
2. Chambers, 53.

Chapter 13

1. Cowman, 243.
2. Ibid., 239.

Chapter 15

1. Michael Card, *A Parable of Joy* (Nashville, Tenn.: Thomas Nelson Publishers, 1995), 103-105. Michael Card's rendering of John 8:1-11.
2. Ibid., 107.
3. Ibid., 104.
4. Chambers, 366.

Chapter 16

1. Chambers, 336.
2. Henry Blackaby, *Experiencing God* (Nashville, Tenn.: Lifeway Press, 1990), 19.
3. Chambers, 129.
4. Cowman, 140.
5. Chambers, 58.
6. A. W. Tozer, *The Pursuit of God* (Camp Hill, Pa.: Christian Publication, 1993), 23.

MORE TITLES BY ERIC AND LESLIE LUDY FROM MULTNOMAH PUBLISHERS

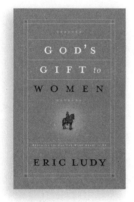

GOD'S GIFT TO WOMEN

In a culture that exalts the caveman-like qualities of masculinity, most women have stopped expecting anything more. Young men are taught to view women as slaves to their self-centered desires. More than ever, men need to know that they can rise above this sad mediocrity. They desperately need someone to recognize their potential for blending courage and kindness, strength and spiritual sensitivity. With its riveting vision of Christ-centered manhood, *God's Gift to Women* shows young men how to become the heroic, selfless knight that every woman dreams about.

ISBN 1-59052-272-9
(Available October 2003)

AUTHENTIC BEAUTY

In a world that seeks to destroy all that is princesslike and feminine within her, that mocks her longing for tender romance and exalts the empty charms of a painted face or a perfect figure—can today's young woman dare to long for more? For every young woman who has asked herself that question, this book offers a breathtaking vision of hope. Refreshingly candid and practical, *Authentic Beauty* explores the boundless opportunities God has for a young woman who is willing to let Him shape every aspect of her life.

ISBN 1-59052-268-0

WHEN DREAMS COME TRUE

This daringly real, intensely moving love story gives vision and hope to everyone in search of a love worth waiting for. In their bestseller *When God Writes Your Love Story*, Eric and Leslie Ludy describe the breathtaking perfection of God's plans for each young person and offer fresh guidelines for being Christlike in relationships with the opposite sex. *When Dreams Come True* shares the Ludys' personal story, illustrating how they lived out the principles of the first book in their own romance and marriage.

ISBN 1-59052-303-2

MUSIC FROM ERIC AND LESLIE LUDY

Faithfully $15.99

Sample Lyrics on the Following Page
Music Available At:

www.loyalpublishing.com
(888) 775-6925

FAITHFULLY (the song)

Written and performed by Eric and Leslie Ludy

Tonight I saw a shooting star • Made we wonder where you are • For years I have been dreaming of you • And I wonder if you're thinking of me too • In this world of cheap romance • And love that only fades after the dance • They say that I'm a fool to wait for something more • How can I really love someone I've never seen before • But I have longed for true love every day that I have lived • And I know that real love is all about learning how to give • So I pray that God will bring you to me • And I pray you'll find me waiting faithfully •• CHORUS •• Faithfully, I am yours • From now until forever • Faithfully, I will write • Write you a love song with my life • 'Cause this kind of love's worth waiting for • No matter how long it takes I am yours • Faithfully •• Tonight I saw two lovers kiss • Reminded me of my own loneliness • They say that I'm a fool to keep praying for you • How can I give up pleasure for a dream that won't come true • But I will keep believing that God still has a plan • And though I cannot see you now, I know that He can • Until I find you, I'll be waiting faithfully

From Eric and Leslie's new CD, *Faithfully*

FAR BEYOND By Leslie

I hear it in a love song or see it on a movie screen • the kind of perfect love story that I have always dreamed • would somehow come into my life • and yet it seems so out of reach • it's all that I think about sometimes • will I ever find a love that's meant to be • maybe these thoughts seem foolish • to a holy God who made the sea and land • but You were the One that created • love between a woman and a man • and deep inside I hear You say • You see all my hopes and fears • and if I give to You the pen of my life • you'll write a tale that all Heaven can cheer •• (chorus) •• far beyond my deepest heart's desire • far beyond what I could ever dream • far beyond my fairy tale imagination • is Your perfect plan for me • there's no limit to romance in all its beauty • when the Author of love shapes my destiny • far beyond the most that I could long for • I will find the dreams You have dreamed for me •• I could search forever • I could look for true love everywhere • if all my dreams were answered • they still could not compare • to the beauty of Your ways • and all plans for my life • 'cause you've been scripting out a story for me • before the very foundations of time

MORE THAN FLOWERS By Eric

what will it be like • to spend life at your side • I'm eager to say I do • and share my life with you • I want our love to be something sweet and heavenly • moving angels to tears • with its simple purity • I want our love to shine • be the romance of all time • one that lives love louder • because it's shown with more than flowers •• (chorus) •• I want you to see me • living out my love for you daily • I want you to hear me adoring you with every word that I speak • I want you to catch me • serving you in ways you weren't supposed to see • it's then you'll know • far more than flowers could ever show •• what will it be like to never say goodbye • to hold you every night • to love you with my life • I want our love to be • a taste of eternity • a picture of God's grace • a reflection of His face • I want our love to glow • demonstrate and show • God's eternal power • shown with more than flowers